The Jesus Tribe

Grace stories from Congo's Mennonites

1912–2012

The Jesus Tribe

Grace stories from Congo's Mennonites

1912–2012

A Project of Africa Inter-Mennonite Mission

Editors
Rod Hollinger-Janzen, Nancy J. Myers, and Jim Bertsche

Authors
Vincent Ndandula, Jean Félix Chimbalanga,
Jackson Beleji, Jim Bertsche,
and Charity Eidse Schellenberg

Library of Congress Cataloging-in-Publication Data

100 ans de mission Mennonite en république démocratique du Congo. English.
The Jesus tribe : grace stories from Congo's Mennonites 1912-2012 : a project of Africa Inter-Mennonite Mission / editors, Rod Hollinger-Janzen, Nancy J. Myers, Jim Bertsche ; authors, Vincent Ndandula ... [et al.].
p. cm.
ISBN 0-936273-49-6 (alk. paper)
1. Mennonites—Missions—Congo (Democratic Republic) 2. Mennonite Church—Missions—History—20th century. I. Hollinger-Janzen, Rod. II. Myers, Nancy J. III. Bertsche, Jim, 1921- IV. Mulebo Ndandula, Vincent. V. Title.
BV3625.C6A1514 2012
266'.976751--dc23

2012023141

THE JESUS TRIBE: GRACE STORIES FROM CONGO'S MENNONITES 1912–2012

Copublished with Institute for the Study of Global Anabaptism, Goshen College, Goshen, IN 46526

Published in collaboration with Mennonite Church of Congo, Evangelical Mennonite Church of Congo, and Africa Inter-Mennonite Mission. Published simultaneously in a Congolese edition as *100 Ans de Mission Mennonite en République Démocratique du Congo : Témoignages des Apports Locaux : 1912–2012.*

Library of Congress Catalog Card Number: 2012023141

International Standard Book Number: 0-936273-49-6
Printed by Evangel Press, Nappanee, Indiana
Book design by Nekeisha Alexis-Baker

To order or request information, phone 1-574-535-0077

To the glory of God,
in recognition of God's grace at work
in the Democratic Republic of Congo
over one hundred years.

❧ Lament for Congo

Only God knows how often I lament the fate of my people; the Congolese people. I know this to be a shared lament of many expatriates of Congolese descent living in diaspora. Thirteen years of abuse and brutal extortions under the inhuman rule of Leopold II, king of the Belgians; fifty-two years of paternalistic governance of the Belgians during the colonial era; five years of the chaotic First Republic that was characterized by civil wars; thirty-two years of repression during the unruly dictatorship of Mobutu Sese Seko; and today life under the formal trappings of a democratic republic that is, in reality, a personal fiefdom of the powers to be: all this has created a peculiar culture in Congo, a left-behind culture that is looked down on by many around the world. There are those, in civil society, the academic world, and even in the church body, who find pleasure in spreading bad tidings about Congo. Here, we are—finally—holding in our hands a book that gives us a different picture, the true picture of the people of Congo, and especially of our Mennonite brothers and sisters and of the good mission workers who evangelized them. The Congolese, Americans, and Canadians who have authored and edited this book of stories offer us images of good and honest Congolese Mennonites who work hard, enjoy life, suffer setbacks, but still hope. They give us the image of Christians who strive to be beacons of hope for a new Congo and signposts for the Kingdom to come. Read this book and you will rediscover the refreshing power of Christianity and the beauty of Christian mission work.

—Hippolyto Tshimanga

❧ Contents

Part II—Christians caught in violence

Part III—A church grows from the ashes

❧ Foreword

Mennonites in Congo: Looking toward the second century

In 1911–12, thirty-three years after the arrival of the first Protestant missionaries in our country, God raised a call among American Mennonites in two small Illinois groups to send pioneers to the interior of our country to announce the good news. Today, this first century of contacts with the Christian world through American Mennonite missionaries has marked our way of being in the world and has left traces that can be seen in former mission stations.

It is essential for the churches born of the Congo Inland Mission, now called Africa Inter-Mennonite Mission (CIM/AIMM), to take another look at their history. Although this history seems distant to some Congolese populations, it is nevertheless a component of the heritage that the Mennonite Church of Congo (CMCo) and the Evangelical Mennonite Church of Congo (CEM) have in common. These churches face challenges represented by evangelization of cultures, the promotion of justice, the struggle for development, the defense of peace, and the search for the ways of democracy. While Congolese Mennonite churches cannot rely entirely on their past for direction, a review of our history will help us accomplish the mission of the church in this third millennium.

The Mennonite mission was dedicated to announcing the word of God and publishing Christian literary works destined for the inhabitants of the evangelized territory, with the goal of forming an autonomous Anabaptist Mennonite church. It was also occupied with education in order to form an intellectual elite. In the health sector, the mission established its work in hospitals, dispensaries, maternities, and leprosariums throughout the mission stations, and it trained nurses to work in them. The missionaries even created co-operatives to promote farming for the good of the local population.

All these accomplishments testify to the greatness of the missionaries' spirit of sacrifice and their care for training and improving the social welfare of the Congolese. We owe our gratitude to them for this work of great breadth.

From 1960 to today, the question of the autonomy of the churches has been linked to historical changes in Africa. The political movement toward independence and the precipitous upsets in the Belgian colonial regime showed that the time was also ripe for profound changes at the level of the congregation. The political situation influenced the vision not only of the Congolese but also of the leaders of the mission.

In February 1960, just four months before Belgium suddenly granted independence, Congolese and missionary delegates met at Ndjoko Punda (the site of the first Mennonite mission) in a "conference of integration," to define processes for the Congolese church to gain autonomy and for mission assistance to continue. As a result of this meeting, the local church was born and took the name Evangelical Mennonite Church of Congo.

Former missionary and historian Jim Bertsche said in a November 2011 interview, "It is important to emphasize that the missionaries did not feel they had the right to name the church; the name 'Mennonite' is the doing of the Congolese." He added that the name was chosen by Mathieu Kazadi, first president of the new church, who said, "We know you very well. You are American Mennonites; you are our parents and we are your children. This church will be called the Evangelical Mennonite Church of Congo."

Missionaries promised the church continued support in funds and missionary personnel as long as deemed necessary and according to the capacity of the Mennonites supporting the mission in North America.

Satisfied with obtaining this autonomy, the Congolese courageously met in Nyanga in August 1960, after the missionaries had been forced to flee because of the independence troubles. This general assembly of the new Evangelical Mennonite Church of Congo put in place a first indigenous leadership team.

When the missionaries returned to Congo in 1961, they and the Congolese agreed that the Congolese were not ready to direct the work of their church entirely by themselves. Two missionaries joined a collegial leadership team: Vernon Sprunger as assistant legal representative, and Arthur Janz as assistant treasurer. The presence of these two missionaries contributed to the church's good operation.

In February–March 1970 a session of the General Assembly of the Protestant Council of Congo was held in Kinshasa. An outcome of this general assembly was a solemn declaration by the majority of the members of this nonprofit association dissolving the missions as institutions separate from the church.

With the end of the missionary institutions in Congo, many discussions took place on the relation between the church planted in a foreign culture and the mission or mother church. Terms such as *fusion, partnership, mutuality, interdependence,* and *internationalization* were offered to describe the future relationship. The Église du Christ au Congo (ECC—Church of Christ in Congo), now the umbrella organization of the unified Protestant churches, adopted the term *fusion,* and the Mennonites followed suit.

The process of fusion of these two organizations, the mission and the local church, which began in 1960, was solidified at the general conference held in June 1971 at Nyanga, and a new leadership team was put in place. All the properties, institutions, and programs of the mission were transferred to the local church, as was the responsibility for the Mennonite mission in the country. In the course of this same year the church name changed to "Communauté Mennonite du Zaïre" (CMZa, now CMCo, for Mennonite Church of Congo). By this time, as the stories in this collection will make clear, a group of refugees fleeing post-independent violence had formed a second Mennonite group in south Kasai. This group now adopted the name "Communauté Evangélique Mennonite," or CEM (Evangelical Mennonite Church).[1]

The end of collegial management was sanctioned by the departure of the last American missionary, Herman Buller, from the management of the CMCo in 1978. This second return of the Mennonite

1 "Communauté" in these names signifies the unity of Protestant churches in Congo: each denomination is a "community" of the Church of Christ in Congo.

missionaries to their country of origin raised more administrative as well as financial difficulties. Certain indigenous administrations who have directed the church from 1978 to today have failed to understand the true meaning of autonomy. During this period of indigenous church leadership, AIMM, despite its determination to reduce subsidies—adopted in October 1980—was still engaged in helping the community financially as much as was necessary.

Today, however, the CMCo and the CEM are going concerns and from now on are obliged to take charge of themselves, albeit in global partnership with the larger Mennonite family. This raises the question of how we should approach the next century.

This is no time to rest. Our second century will not be at all like today. We live already in the prelude to these changes. Great technological advances are shaping the North, but few are operating in the South of the planet. This hemisphere in which the Mennonite work has been planted lags behind. Nevertheless we live on the same planet. The problems of the South will be felt in the North as well. What will be our response to the accelerated degradation of the environment and the scandalous impoverishment of the countries most touched by economic and food crises? We face many unknowns. We are in a new world that requires a different perception and understanding of modernity.

In the past, our missionaries began the work of evangelization and church life with health and education. And since 1960 the autonomous Mennonite church has continued this work and by the grace of God has participated in the life of the Congolese population with the limited means bequeathed by the missionaries in these domains.

Technology has always been important to the church's mission. If I am not mistaken, the Mennonites were the first to install, in 1951, a shortwave radio network connecting their stations. This greatly improved communications and efficiency. Before this new communication technology, people walked or rode bicycles over great distances in order to have contact. The technology also played an important role in evangelization.

Today the Mennonite churches that were formed from CIM/AIMM have no media through which they can announce the good news. The majority of our congregations even lack sound systems, although we know that music contributes to evangelization, attracts attention and crowds, and brings peace and joy. The Mennonite primary and secondary schools are not equipped with libraries and computers. The central offices of the church are not linked to the Internet.

The church has not done much to modernize the medical service of the church with its web of dispensaries, health centers, and general referral hospitals. The health of the population is the backbone of all development and an incontrovertible factor in evangelization centered on development and modernization. It is imperative that in the next century we give it first place. The offer of quality healthcare (continuous, integrated, universal, effective, and efficient) in these Mennonite structures requires modern biomedical equipment: sonograms, scanners, well-equipped operating rooms, surgical and maternity equipment, and so forth. This network must contribute to the struggle against the modern worldwide plagues, which particularly affect Congo: HIV/AIDS, malaria, and tuberculosis.

The mechanization of agriculture and the modernization of animal husbandry are proven priorities. Our leaders must be broadly trained. The church must educate pastors not only in theology but also in scientific domains such as the environment, social sciences, land law, and medicine and health. Our hope, too, is that our private Mennonite schools can be modernized. Because of a lack of effective training in faith and Christian ethics at the primary and secondary levels, our children are vulnerable to the influences of other religions and occultism they encounter in Congolese university environments.

Today we are part of a great worldwide Mennonite family. Love and respect should animate our relations, along with the desire for the edification of the church, so that it continues in the service of people and efforts to aid the poor. Look at how our partner Catholic agencies work with their churches in the South. The unilateral mission, that is to say, the one that separates North from South, is over. All the churches must evangelize together.

Congolese Mennonite Anabaptism must be understood according to our culture. There are many valuable aspects of Congolese culture conveyed in its music, proverbs, tales, philosophy, the place it gives to blood sacrifices, the concept of what is taboo and what is holy, the idea of humans set apart by God, its sense of hierarchy, and its innate religious spirit, as well as the value Africans give to nonviolence, unity, peace, and reconciliation. All of that can be developed to solidify Congolese Mennonites' faith in Jesus Christ. They will discover a type of church that loves the Lord with all its heart, mind, strength, and soul. They will discover a holy, united church in which the gifts of each one will be exercised for the good of the whole body of Christ.

Today is already the future. We must act now! What Mennonite Church in Congo will we leave to posterity? What is our role today? Let's act together, at the same time, to give a new breath of evangelization and mission to the Mennonite work in Congo. As we say, referring to our staple dish, "It takes at least two fingers to hold the *fufu*!"

Our ardent desire for the second century stays focused on evangelization and mission by new methods, and on support for the well-being and economic development of our people. In this way the church will be a positive influence, an inspiration, a proponent of new ways, a conscience in society.

François Tshidimu
Pastor, Bondeko Mennonite Church, Kinshasa
Chair, Centennial Reception Committee

❧ Editors' preface

Early in 2009 this book was only a dream, and a fragile one at that. Africa Inter-Mennonite Mission's centennial year, 2012, was just around the corner. It was time to start planning a celebration. A hundred years of unbroken Mennonite presence and witness in Congo was indeed noteworthy.

Discussion quickly took off in a variety of directions. We could trace the incredible international missionary team that the Lord put together across a century. We could show the evolving history of a growing inter-Mennonite mission venture, which eventually brought together a partnership of six different North American Mennonite conferences in common mission and service in that distant land.

There were statistics by the bucketful: numbers of students graduated, healthy babies born, successful surgeries performed, teachers and pastors trained, and above all, baptized believers who, at the century mark, constitute a Congolese Mennonite community whose three branches include approximately 225,000 members.[1]

But as historically important as these numbers are, they fall short of an essential point. We had the growing conviction that the focus of centennial celebrations needed somehow to take the form of a tribute to the life-changing impact of God's grace on countless lives across a century.

1 Stories in this book come principally from two branches, the Mennonite Church of Congo and the Evangelical Mennonite Church of Congo. See the appendix, "Mennonite church names."

Thus was born the idea of a project to gather stories—stories by Africans about Africans who had faith-based, life-changing encounters with Jesus and who then became evangelists of their own people, planters of their own churches, and witnesses to God's grace in their lives.

The hurdles were high. Time was already short for such an undertaking. Were there Congolese who could be trained and equipped on short notice to fan out across an area the size of the state of Illinois, among several different ethnic groups, to seek out and document such stories? Soon enough there would be another problem, of finding African writers who knew the local tribal languages in which the raw material was recorded and who were competent to turn these biographical records into good French stories. To further complicate the picture, we wanted not just a French story collection as a centennial gift to the Congo Mennonite churches but also an English version for distribution here in North America. Could we assemble the necessary translation and editorial team on this end?

And finally, the story-gathering project was taking shape during a major economic slump in the United States. Were there people prepared to join us in our vision and support of a project that would require more than $120,000?

One by one, each seemingly insurmountable hurdle was cleared, many of them just in time to meet a series of urgent deadlines: the book that you hold in your hands is itself something of a miracle.

As you read, please note the following features of the story collection:

- They are presented in roughly chronological order and scattered across a hundred years. To a prodigious collection of stories gathered by Congolese researchers and writers, in the English edition we have added a number written by longtime missionary Jim Bertsche, because they offer valuable background for North American readers.
- The profiles and stories come from a mix of at least eight ethnic groups. They are about men and women, youth and older folks, people who are literate and semi-literate, North Americans and Congolese, city dwellers and rural village folk, the living and the dead.
- They reflect courage and amazing faith amid enormous cultural pressures. They present an honest account of these

pressures and people's struggles with them. They portray an African interpretation of basic Anabaptist belief in peace, nonviolence, and forgiveness.

- In a society that has been racked by periodic violence, these stories constitute a book of martyrs in the Congo Mennonite family, as well as a compendium of elders who have lived long and fruitful lives in the church.
- For North American readers, these stories constitute a primer in the simple practice of prayer, the life-changing impact of scripture and song, and the art of walking humbly by faith and not by sight.

Readers may be curious about our chosen title, *The Jesus Tribe.* It emerges out of one of the stories recorded here. In a situation of tribal conflict, Pastor Charles Kwamba is asked to choose sides. His reply? "I have become a member of the Jesus tribe." This response was a powerful witness to the peace and unity for which Jesus prayed, a way for Kwamba to say that his identity was no longer primarily with his blood ancestral group but with an intertribal church—the Jesus Tribe. The theme of overcoming tribal barriers out of love for Jesus and commitment to his intertribal family is a major theme throughout the book.

As additional guides we have added maps and an appendix defining some terms and offering history and background on such things as church practices, structures, and names.

We trust that the French collection will help today's Congolese Mennonites gain a new understanding of the shoulders they stand on. We trust that the English collection will help the North American Mennonite community gain a vivid sense of their brothers and sisters in Congo and inspire reflection on an ancient scriptural affirmation: "It is not by might nor by power but by my Spirit, says the Lord."

Part I
Letters, numbers, and Yesu

1 ❧ A Mennonite evangelist tied to a corpse

In January 1912 a pioneering trio of missionaries rode a boat up the Kasai River in central Congo as far as they could go.[1] Arriving at Wissman Falls, they disembarked, pitched tents, and began the arduous labor of establishing the first mission post of Congo Inland Mission. Drawing on the name of the local area, they called the post Ndjoko Punda.

The only Protestant missionaries for miles in any direction, Lawrence and Rose Boehning Haigh and Alvin Stevenson were starting from scratch. Everything needed to be done at once: arranging for help from the nearby villages, tackling the local Tshiluba language, learning to barter for food, and building the first temporary shelters and a small place of worship out of thatch and sticks.

The missionaries knew they would succeed in planting the church of Christ in the area only if they could win and train Africans to become the messengers of the good news to their own people. An early strategy was to open simple schools to which they invited anyone interested in learning how to read and write in their own language. The first students were mostly boys in their early teens

---

photo—David Lupera, one of the early primary school students described in this story

1 This story is preserved as it was told to Jim Bertsche by Pastor David. Unfortunately, the names of the evangelist and his wife have been lost in the transmission of the story.

and young men in their twenties. Some soon tired of the strange activities and drifted back to village life, but others were captivated by the marvel of learning how to read and write. And then they began to hear a strange new story about someone called Yesu, the very son of the creating God who had come to give his life through his own sacrificial death on a cross for them.

It took about three years before the missionaries felt some African believers were ready to be baptized. They then opened a simple Bible school for these students, with concentrated study of scriptures in Tshiluba provided by the large Presbyterian mission that was their neighbor to the east.

The Mennonite missionaries would take the Bible school students with them into the surrounding villages, where they held open-air meetings. In this way the students learned how to preach and to hold conversations with individuals who wanted to hear more.

In the late 1920s the missionaries began to challenge the Bible school students to become resident evangelists in outlying villages. By this time the schools were attracting a few village girls who, as they came to know Jesus as their Savior, also came to know the young men and became their wives.

By the early 1930s a number of couples resided in villages around the station, but there was a growing sense of urgency to place at least one couple among a large tribe to the west, known as the Bashilele or Lele. A proud ironworking tribe, the Lele were excellent hunters and had consistently resisted all the missionaries' efforts to get a hearing for the gospel. Meanwhile, a devoted young couple had finished the station Bible school and declared their desire to be "Jesus people" in a village. Impressed by their warmth and devotion, the missionaries asked them to be the first couple to be placed among the Lele people. "With the Lord's help, we are willing," they said.

A village was chosen, and a missionary and the young couple sought out the local chief. "Why would we want a mission teacher?" the chief asked. "What does he know that we need to know? Could we hunt better if he lived here? Could we smelt iron better than our forefathers if he talked about Yesu among us?"

Finally the village leaders gave grudging agreement, on condition that the couple would establish their home at the very edge of the village. No help would be given them to build their first thatch-

and-stick shelter or to put out their first fields. Nor would the villagers send any children to the school the couple talked about starting.

Slowly the couple settled in. They tied a piece of scrap iron to a tree and beat it each morning to call children to school. But the chief was as good as his word: they received no help, and no children came to school. Although they often sat with the chief and his elders, explaining what they hoped to do, they were met with stony indifference. On Sunday the couple always came to the open area in the middle of the village, called people to gather, sang songs, and then told them stories about Yesu.

One day the village chief summoned the evangelist and posed a series of questions. The conversation went something like this:

"You keep telling us about someone named Yesu."

"That's true."

"You tell us that he raised people from the dead while he was on earth."

"He did."

"You say that he himself died and then three days later rose from his grave."

"He did."

"Well, we want to try this Yesu business out here in our village today. Do you see that corpse over there? That man died this past night. Today at sundown, we will bury him as is our custom. But since your Yesu can raise dead people back to life, we want to see that happen before our eyes today. We're going to tie you to that corpse. Then you can ask your Yesu to bring him back to life. If he does, we will rejoice and we'll believe in your Yesu. But if not, we'll put you in the grave along with him."

They tied the evangelist on top of the dead body. The chief and his elders then sat under nearby palm trees, watching. Occasionally someone would call out to the evangelist, asking whether there was any sign of life in the dead man under him.

Time passed and sundown approached. Just then a boy came running, all out of breath. The Belgian administrator for the area was in the next village and was coming their way! This prompted an explosion of activity. Someone hurried to the corpse and cut the evangelist free. Soon there was the sound of a vehicle approaching along the nearby road. In the confusion the evangelist slipped away and joined his anxious wife in their little hut at the edge of the village.

Back in the village the colonial official greeted the chief and his elders. "And how are things here? I hear that you now have a mission teacher. How is he?"

"Oh yes. As a matter of fact we were just with him here a moment ago."

"I do not have time now, but next visit I'll stay longer," the official promised.

As he left, the chief and his elders exchanged sly glances and smiles. They were confident that by morning the evangelist and his wife would be gone.

Back in their little shelter the teacher-evangelist and his wife reviewed the experiences of the day. "What now?" they wondered. "If we gather up our few belongings into two bundles and start walking, by daylight we can be nearly halfway back to the mission station. But if we do that, what will we tell the missionaries? What will we tell our fellow Christians? We were sent here to tell these people about Yesu and not a single person has accepted him. And we don't have a single student for our school."

After a long silence they prayed together and decided that no matter what lay ahead for them, they had to stay.

Next morning, as the sun came up, the astonished chief and his people heard the familiar sound of the teacher hitting his piece of iron with a stone, summoning the children to school.

In the village a group of boys heard the distant sound of stone on iron. One of them told the others: "We thought that after what our fathers did to the teacher yesterday, they would run away in the night. But there he is, inviting us like always. If they are still here in our village after the way we treated them, they must have something important to tell us, and I'm going to find out what it is." Following his lead, several other boys joined him.

In time, that boy—David Lupera—became the first ordained minister from the Lele tribe.

Jim Bertsche

2 ❧ I just did what Jesus said

Badibanga appeared one day at the new mission post, Ndjoko Punda. Like other boys of the area, he was attracted by the news that he could enroll in a school started by the white-skinned people and learn *maleta ne manomba,* letters and numbers.

Badibanga quickly proved himself an apt student with a hunger to learn. Although his home village was several kilometers from the mission post, he was always at school on time, soaking up how to spell out words with strange marks on a blackboard and, with equally strange marks, add up sums without counting fingers even once.

Badibanga listened just as attentively when he began to hear the story of Jesus. In time he decided to invite Christ into his heart and life, and when he did so, it was with a total commitment to this new relationship. He became a *mwena Yesu,* a Jesus person.

One Sunday morning during his last year of school he joined a group of other students as they made their way down the hill to the Kasai River and gave public witness to their faith by baptism. In the custom of the African church, in the process he adopted a new name, Valentin.

As graduation time neared, Valentin one day explained to the missionary director his great desire to seek training as a clerk. Anyone who could type, keep books, and oversee the filing of letters and documents could find immediate employment either in government offices or with Portuguese commercial men of the area. If he could do that, he'd be able to help his large family back in his home village and also have money to give to his church. No such training was available at Ndjoko Punda, but another mission post far downstream offered it. His grades were good; would the missionary write on his behalf and seek an opening in their school? The director agreed. One day the riverboat brought a mail sack containing a letter of acceptance.

Carefully guarding his acceptance letter, Valentin boarded a riverboat that September, and after nearly two days of travel he disembarked down the hill from the Baptist mission post. He was shown to the boys dorm and given a bed. He unrolled his blanket and put his little bundle of belongings underneath.

The other boys in the dorm soon discovered they had a stranger among them, and Valentin became the object of harassment. "Where are you from? Why are you here? You don't even speak our language! We don't want you here. Go back where you came from!"

And so it went, day in and day out. But Valentin Badibanga did not retaliate in anger. He simply kept his peace and tried to stay out of the way of his tormenters.

One day he came to the dorm from class to find that his bed had been thrown out into the yard, upside down. His blanket lay beside it on the ground, all stained with ink. Valentin did not shout; he did not go to the school principal to complain. He simply gathered his things and pulled his bamboo cot back into the dorm to the far end where he had been isolated. He had come to study to be a clerk, and this was what he determined to do, no matter what.

A few days later the school principal called a meeting of all of the boys in the school. He explained that a woman from a far-off village had been carried into the station hospital the night before because she needed help to give birth to her baby. The doctor helped her, but she had lost so much blood before she arrived that unless she had a transfusion she would die. The missionary explained that they had already tested the blood of all of the medical staff and the missionaries, but no one had the same type as the village woman who was dying. He asked if any students would be willing to have their blood type tested. And in the event that someone had the right type, would he be willing to give some of his blood to save the life of the village woman?

There was a long silence. All sorts of thoughts were going through the minds of the boys. "Give my blood? For someone I don't even know? If I give my blood, won't I get sick or maybe even die?"

Still the missionary waited. Suddenly there was a voice at the back of the room, the voice of Valentin. "I'm willing," he said.

Shamed by this example of compassion by someone not of their tribe, slowly others said they too would be willing to be tested.

As it turned out, Valentin did not have the right blood type, but a donor was found among other volunteers. The woman was given the transfusion she desperately needed, her life was saved, and in a few weeks she returned to her home village with a healthy baby.

When the first year of study came to a close, the principal handed Valentin a letter to take to the Mennonite missionaries at Ndjoko Punda. Valentin stopped by the missionary's home and reported that his first year of study had gone well. "I'm learning exactly what I want to know. With another year, I'll have my certificate and I'll be able to look for a job."

Valentin dropped off the letter and hurried off to his home village. The missionary opened the letter and learned what Valentin had done for the woman in need. At the first opportunity he called for Valentin and said, "We are amazed at your Christian witness and thank the Lord for you."

Valentin Badibanga responded, "I don't understand why all of you missionaries are so surprised. When I was here in school learning about Jesus, I read one day that he told his followers to do to others as they'd like them to do to them. Isn't that what the Bible says? Well, that's all I did. I just did what Jesus said!"

Jim Bertsche

3 ⁂ The price was too high

Maliya and Davidi[1] were new young Christians who had gone through the Ndjoko Punda mission school and been baptized. When approached by the missionaries about entering the little two-year Bible school, they both readily accepted. By this time they had moved from their home villages to the station, where they lived in the dorms.

As they sat together in the same classes day by day, they began to take note of each other. At the end of their two years of study, Davidi proposed marriage to Maliya through his village elders. After an appropriate dowry had been agreed on by the clan elders of the two young people, a wedding was planned for the station chapel in the presence of Christians as well as village friends and relatives.

Before the wedding ceremony, Maliya and Davidi had been given instruction on the meaning of Christian marriage and were told that they would be called on to make public commitments to faithfulness to each other in the sight of God and all those present. They readily agreed to do so.

After Davidi's trial period of teaching one of the primary classes on the station and taking his turn preaching in morning chapels, he and Maliya were asked by a missionary and an African pastor whether they would be willing to go to a village, begin a simple school for village children, and tell the village folk about Jesus. If they accepted,

1 The real names of the couple involved have regrettably been lost in the transmission of their story across four generations.

they would be the first Christians ever to live in that village. They were told that it would not be easy and that they might have to work for a long while before they brought anyone to faith in Jesus. They would surely be tempted by the non-Christian ways about them and would need to commit themselves to the Lord daily for guidance, strength, and wisdom for their assignment.

Their response was humble, but direct. "We were born in the sort of villages you are talking about. We know the ways of those who know nothing about Jesus and his love. We know very well that we alone cannot bring people to Jesus. But if you here at the mission post promise to pray for us every day, we are willing to go."

A village was found where the chief agreed to accept them. They immediately went to work. Maliya needed to plant fields to feed herself and her husband. Davidi made many trips into the surrounding bush to cut poles and thatch grass to build their simple home and then a little shelter which would serve as both a school and—one day—a chapel.

A few months after their arrival, Maliya told her husband that she wanted to go to the small store along the road at the edge of their village. She had saved a few coins and thought she had enough money to buy a piece of cotton fabric to use as a wraparound skirt. Davidi responded that if she had enough money, she should go.

Maliya entered the store, greeted the paunchy, middle-aged storekeeper, and told him what she was looking for. Looking her over, he commented that he had not seen her in his store before. She explained that she and her husband had arrived in the village only a few months earlier and that they had come to start a school and to tell the people about Jesus.

"Ah, that's good," he responded. He placed several bolts of brightly colored cotton prints on the counter. After looking them over she chose one pattern and asked for a piece two meters in length.

He folded the piece and laid it before her. When she asked how much she owed, he replied: "Oh, you don't need to pay for the cloth today. Just take it. Enjoy it. The next time you come to my store we can discuss your bill."

Still in her teens and married less than a year, she instinctively knew that the ingratiating clerk was seeking to lay a trap for her. If she followed through on his proposal, she knew that when she returned he would invite her to join him in the little shuttered room at the back of the store to "settle her account."

Turning on her heel, she left the folded cloth lying on the counter and returned to her husband empty-handed.

"Didn't you go to purchase a piece of cloth?" he asked.

"Yes, I did."

"Didn't you find anything you liked?"

"Yes, I did."

"Then why didn't you buy it?" Davidi asked.

Maliya replied, "The price was too high."

Jim Bertsche

4 ❧ Please send us that lady with the book

Joseph Nsongamadi and Naomi, his wife, graduated from the two-year Bible school at a moment in the early 1920s when the mission's witness was expanding. Ndjoko Punda had been established in 1912 upon the arrival of the first pioneer trio of missionaries. A second mission post had been located shortly thereafter at Kalamba, some 300 kilometers to the south along the Kasai River. In 1921 a third post was opened among the eastern Pende people adjacent to the village of Nyanga. There was immediate concern to make contact with the western Pende across the Loange River.

Although no American missionaries were available at the time to start a major new post, several missionary men planned an exploratory trek across the river. Before leaving, they asked Nsongamadi and Naomi if they would be willing to go with them and, if a good place for a future mission post was found, stay behind as the first missionaries until additional recruits arrived from America.

Nsongamadi and Naomi could have found many legitimate excuses to stay at Ndjoko Punda. They longed to see their own tribal people come to know Jesus as they had; they found teaching on the station exciting; they did not know the language of the Pende people; they would be the only "Jesus people" there; they would be foreigners and strangers far from home. But after prayer, they accepted this as a call from God.

photo—Naomi with her husband, Joseph Nsongamadi

After trekking for days on foot and crossing a wide river in dugout canoes, they walked still farther until they arrived at a large village called Mukedi. The chief was in charge not only of that village but also of several others in the area. The missionaries sought a hearing with him and explained the purpose of their visit. They said they intended later to place white-skinned missionaries next to his village, but in the meantime, for one year, they were proposing to leave Nsongamadi and Naomi with them.

The chief was not impressed. "Why leave them with us? What will they do here? They are of another tribe. They don't even speak our language. A school? We're not interested. There will be no children from my village available." Grudgingly, however, the chief finally agreed to give them temporary shelter and some food until Nsongamadi could build their own simple shelter out at the edge of the village and Naomi could plant her own gardens. It was amid such uncertainty that the missionary men left them on their own.

A year later, in 1923, a small contingent of American missionaries arrived at Mukedi. They found Nsongamadi and Naomi at their post. Had there been any converts during the year? No, not one, but they had faithfully told the people about Jesus. Did they have a school? Not exactly, but the chief had finally offered to give them a little orphan girl to teach, if they would quit bothering him!

They had faithfully sown seed on what had appeared to be totally sterile ground. The gospel later took root at Mukedi, and in time a large mission post and church were established.

Nsongamadi and Naomi returned with joy to Ndjoko Punda among their own people and quickly merged into the life of the growing Christian community there. He once again became a teacher on the station and a church leader, while she soon demonstrated a great gift for visiting and helping women who were by then coming to the station for medical help or to give birth.

Whenever Naomi made her rounds among the women, she carried her Tshiluba Bible in the crook of her arm. Thumbed and worn, it was a book with which she by then was familiar, one to which she had often turned during that long, difficult year at Mukedi. Mixing readings with her own glowing accounts of the difference Jesus had made in her life, her prayers were warm outpourings of simple conversation with her *Tata Nzambi,* Father God, and always left her sisters at the medical facility with a sense of being cared for and loved.

Then tragedy struck. Nsongamadi had been complaining about pain in his feet as he walked. In time the lesions on his feet were declared to be cancerous. Gradually Naomi's time came to be devoted to the care of her husband on the hospital grounds where he stayed. John and Jeanne Zook, a physician and nurse team, were in charge of the station hospital at that time and became well acquainted with the couple. With limited medication and equipment available to them, they did their best to at least keep the wounds clean and to alleviate pain for this faithful servant of the Lord.

By the time Nsongamadi breathed his last, the Zooks had been transferred to work in a large city hospital in the urban center of Kananga. They soon realized that little was being done for the spiritual comfort and help of the patients. Remembering Naomi back at Djoko, they sent word inviting her to join them in the city. They would see to her board and room and personal expenses. There was endless need and opportunity for her in the halls of the government hospital.

She quickly accepted the invitation and soon became a familiar figure. Even when she was in failing health, Naomi spent her last days in a ministry she loved and at which she excelled, responding to continual requests from up and down the halls: "Please send us that lady with the book."

Jim Bertsche

5 ❦ Frank Enns and Pierre Mazemba, partners in faith

No Mennonite missionary stayed longer at one place than Frank Enns. No partnership between a missionary and a Congolese pastor endured longer than that between Frank Enns and Pierre Mazemba. The Nyanga mission station and the Nyanga church district bear the imprint of these two men.

Born into a devout Mennonite wheat farming family near Inman, Kansas, in 1895, Frank J. Enns nearly walked out on his baptism as a teenager. Although he had declared his faith in Christ and enrolled in a baptismal class, when the time came he abruptly stood and left the church! Pursued by his father and an older brother, he explained that he was not sure he was worthy of baptism. When they explained to him that baptism was not for "worthy" people but rather for people who had accepted Jesus as their Savior, he reentered the church and with the others signaled his trust in Jesus for his salvation.

Initially Frank had no idea of going further in school than his siblings, who had dropped out before the final exams of the primary cycle to give full time to farming activities. However, a perceptive teacher saw his potential, and he eventually went through high school and on to college and a year at Northern Baptist Seminary in Chicago. He married Agnes Neufeld in June 1926, and the couple left for Congo four months later under the auspices of Congo Inland Mission. Their decision had been greatly influenced by Rev. J. P. Bark-

photo—Frank Enns and Pierre Mazemba

man, a pioneer of that new inter-Mennonite mission who visited Kansas during a furlough and let it be known that he wanted to take Frank Enns back with him.

They traveled to Nyanga by train, ocean freighter, train again, riverboat, and finally by *kipoy*, a wicker chair mounted between two long bamboo poles with crossbars and carried by four men. They arrived to find that the resident missionary couple was preparing to leave for furlough. Thus in two weeks time Frank and Agnes found themselves on a mission post which had been planted only three years earlier. A third missionary, Kornelia Unrau, a nurse, had arrived just six months earlier. Language study? They would learn the Pende language (Gipende) on the fly! But help was on the way.

Pierre Mazemba, a stocky teenager of medium height with a face deeply pockmarked by smallpox he had survived as a child, had been sent some five years earlier to Ndjoko Punda, where he and two other Nyanga boys were enrolled in station schools and given Bible training. A few years after the Ennses arrived, the young men returned to Nyanga, sought out Christian girls for marriage, and asked how they could serve the Lord in their home territory.

Enns saw strong pastoral potential in Pierre Mazemba. Over time, the two would forge an enduring bond. And so, among all of the scores of missionaries who served with the Mennonite mission, Frank Enns had the unique experience of being placed at a new station just in process of formation, being reassigned to the same place throughout his entire missionary career, and maintaining a lifelong partnership with a Congolese leader.

During their first term at Nyanga, Frank and Agnes's first child, a son, was born. They named him John, or Yone in Gipende. In the tradition of the Pende people, Frank and Agnes were thereafter known as Sh'a Yone and Gin'a Yone, the father and mother of John.

Agriculture was close to Frank's heart. Early on he had the foresight to secure additional hectares of land adjacent to the mission station. He required every class of students to plant and tend their own garden plot, which helped supply their food during the school year. Eventually a farm was established where experimental crops were planted and a variety of animal husbandry projects were designed to improve the protein content of the local cassava-based diet. Nyanga station eventually became a peaceful oasis amid the rolling scrub bush land around it. Today straight paths laid out at right angles are lined by large mango trees that provide shade and abundant fruit. In other places are coconut palms, nut palms, and a variety of citrus trees.

But Enns's enduring passion was evangelism. As the Belgian government gradually cut roads through the bush country around him, he secured a Model A Ford from the States. Accompanied by Pastor Pierre Mazemba or other African staff, he spent days on end pushing ever farther into the area designated as the Nyanga district of the Congo Inland Mission field for which they were responsible. Sleeping on his camp cot and sharing the evening cassava mush with village Christians, he sat long hours, listened carefully, admonished them with passages of God's word, and prayed with them. No village visit was complete without at least one public meeting with hymns and a message about Jesus.

The Ennses reached retirement age in 1960. Before they departed, the Nyanga Christians arranged a day of celebration and remembrance. Fabricating two kipoys, they installed Frank and Agnes on individual chairs and carried them on a long tour of Nyanga station, commemorating the way the couple had arrived in 1926.

When Nyanga Christians heard of Agnes's death in 1965, they sent an appeal to Frank, "Please come back. Your work among us is not finished." And so he returned to Congo alone for three more years among a people who had become the passion of his heart. He was not content to stay on the station but put together a camping kit and chop box for food and asked to be taken out to various villages and left there for ten days or two weeks. When his visit and ministry was complete in one village, he would get on his bicycle and have village boys carry his sparse luggage, while others put a long forked stick in position under his bike seat and pushed him through the sand to his next destination.

Uncle Frank, as younger missionaries affectionately called him, died in retirement in 1975 surrounded by his bird feeders, his binoculars, and an easel on which he now and again did an oil painting.

When news of his death reached Nyanga, word quickly spread that a traditional *masaga* would be held for Sh'a Yone in front of the house where he had lived for so many years. The masaga is a time of mourning that accompanies all village deaths. Whereas among non-Christians it is a time of wailing and mourning, African Christians have turned it into a time of remembrance and celebration of the home-going of a fellow believer.

In front of the Enns home was a gigantic tree under which Mennonite Central Committee teachers had laid out a tennis court. On the designated evening at sundown, scores of people converged on the spot around a fire. An old chair once used by Enns was found somewhere and placed in a central location. The aging Pastor Mazemba was invited to sit in it.

The night was given to telling stories about Tata Sh'a Yone—something he'd done, taught, said in a sermon, or built; some discipline he'd dispensed; someone he'd married, baptized, or ordained to the ministry—interspersed with the singing of many Gipende hymns.

Finally came Pastor Pierre Mazemba's turn. All leaned forward to hear what form his reminiscing might take, for all knew that no one among them had spent more time with Enns than he. Normally a taciturn man not known for the display of emotion, Mazemba too reviewed some of the places he'd traveled with Enns, some experiences they'd had together, some things he'd learned from him. Finally he concluded: "Sh'a Yone lived his life seeking the lives of others."

He paused. Finally, with tears streaming down his face, he said quietly, "Sh'a Yone, I'm coming."

Jim Bertsche

6 ❧ Death on an evangelism mission

Daniel Kitamba was one of the first three people baptized by the Nyanga mission in 1921. He thus opened the way for many others who would follow. That event, which happened in the first decade of Mennonite evangelization in Congo, takes on particular significance when one knows that his people were situated at the intersection of traditional religion and Christianity.

Daniel was born around 1904. His parents were followers of traditional African religion, firmly believing in the omnipotence of life energies and engaging in a range of worship practices and values that have the goal of guiding and safeguarding the life of their community.

Raised in Ndjoko Punda, he did his primary and biblical studies in the first missionary schools there. In Nyanga he married Ruth Isaka in 1926, the first religious marriage celebrated at the Nyanga mission. Ruth was the daughter of the chief of her husband's village. To this couple were born three boys and three girls.

As a married man, Daniel Kitamba had to find work to support his household. After faithful service as a teacher at all four stations the Mennonite missionaries had opened by then—Ndjoko Punda, Nyanga, Kalamba, and Mukedi—he was employed by the missionaries as a supervisor of the different schools opened in the villages depending on the Nyanga outpost.

---

photo—Daniel Kitamba

Because of his dynamism, dedication, and sense of responsibility, he took part, on behalf of his church, in conferences on teaching organized in the capital city, Leopoldville (now Kinshasa), and in Rhodesia. The church decided to consecrate him as a deacon. His contribution was great in the expansion of the evangelical work of Congo Inland Mission in the large province of Kasai and elsewhere.

But his life was brief. Like Jesus Christ, Daniel Kitamba would spend only three decades on this earth. While he was on a mission of evangelization, this devoted man was struck by lightning on October 5, 1936, in the village of Jimbo Kimbuanda. The church of Nyanga, which had a good opinion of this pioneer, did everything possible, bringing his remains back to Nyanga and finally to the village Kipoko, where he would be buried in honor. Thus ended the short life of a man serving his Lord who died on the battlefield, like a soldier at the front, leaving a widow and six children.

But the story repeats itself in a different way. After his father's death, Daniel Kitamba's eldest son, David Bieng, became active in politics. When the country achieved independence, he was among the people most in the public eye in Kasai. But one morning in the year 1961 he was assassinated at the Tshikapa airport, bringing on another unexpected round of mourning.

It can be said of Daniel Kitamba that he died in the line of duty, practicing his faith. Many have given their lives, freely or forcibly, for ideals other than the Christian faith. But dying for the one who died on the cross because of our sins remains a great sacrifice.

Jackson Beleji

7 ❧ One of the first Christians at Mukedi

David Djoko was born around the turn of the century in the region of Mukedi. He was one of the first eight Christians to be baptized by immersion, according to Anabaptist rites, in the Tshinyo River. It was 1927. These eight were to be the nucleus of evangelization in the Mukedi region.

Among the first to receive a certificate from the Bible school at Mukedi, in 1932, David became one of the first teacher-evangelists sent from the mission. In 1937 he changed careers and went to work for the Equatorial Kasai Company, the large Belgian company that controlled the palm oil trade in the area. He married Rebecca Kwango, and they had eleven children.

Thanks to good training and advice, these children all became Christians and were drawn to responsible positions in different sectors. Despite material comforts resulting from their position in society, and thanks to the education received from their father, these children never neglected the word of God, which edifies and fortifies believers. David himself, although working for a large company, never stopped evangelizing the workers who were under his orders.

He gave up the contract with the company, however, and took up studies again. This time he went to the mission's teacher training institute and obtained a higher teaching certificate in 1940. This second degree enabled him to embrace another career, as a secretary

photo—David Djoko

in the administration of Chief Nzamba of Bakwa Katundo. He served there for two years. During the exercise of his functions, David was appreciated by the chief for his efficiency, openness, alertness, and dignity. He settled all the complaints presented to him with justice.

After two years he went back to the mission post, where once again he demonstrated his devotion and unconditional attachment to his employers. In response, the missionaries conferred on him the responsibility of overseeing the female students who were housed in the mission dormitories. David fulfilled this task appropriately and conscientiously as a good Christian, firm in his positions but also exhibiting a well-developed ability to listen. He always abstained from personal disputes and remained submitted to his church.

Although certain young people had been trained especially to teach Sunday school, David Djoko was without doubt the best Sunday school teacher in the district. In addition, one could see in him an elevated sense of consideration for everybody.

David Djoko died at the Mukedi mission in 2003. He was believed to be more than 100 years old.

Jackson Beleji

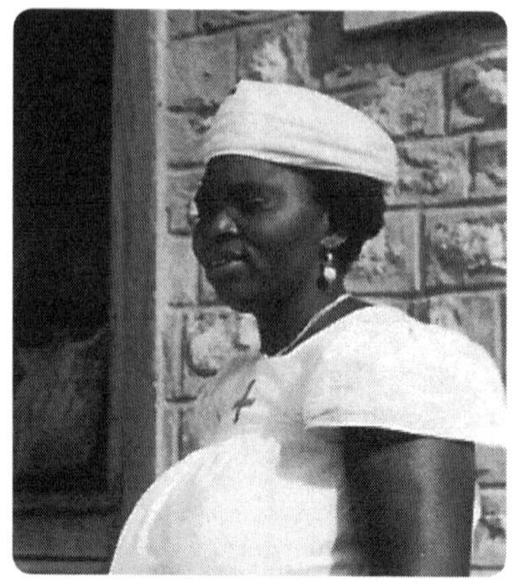

8 ❧ Rebecca, Jacob, and a son named Samuel

Rebecca Gavunji was abandoned twice when she was very young. She was born in 1923 in the village of Lubu Kakese. Her mother died after the birth. Members of her mother's family did not want to assume responsibility for the baby and decided to place her in the coffin with her deceased mother so that she would be buried along with her.

Mennonite missionaries, accompanied by Pastor Joseph Nsongamadi[1] were passing through the village exactly at that time and found the people mourning. Learning about the circumstances, they asked the members of that family to give them the child. The family relinquished the child to the missionaries for their care at the mission station.

Several years later, the missionaries needed to go on leave to the United States, and the little girl was returned to her grandfather's care in the village. One day the wife of Rebecca's grandfather took her along with her into the countryside, where the little girl's leg was injured. The woman abandoned her and returned to the village. A good-hearted mother passing by found the child crying, with a large wound on her leg. This good Samaritan tied up the wound and helped the child get back to the village. From there she was taken to the mis-

---

photos—Rebecca Gavunji and Jacob Gasala

1 See "Please send us that lady with the book" (chapter 4).

sion and restored to the care of the missionaries, who had returned by then. Rebecca was six years old.

Finally it was decided to send the girl to Ndjoko Punda to the orphanage. It was at the Ndjoko Punda orphanage that she began to work in the capacity of "room girl" or nurse's aide. She was baptized in Mukedi in 1934 and married Jacob Gasala in 1935. She became, in Mukedi, a midwife and then director of the maternity clinic from 1949 to 1972. The maternity clinic of Mukedi, which still exists, is named for her, the Mama Gavunji Maternity Clinic.

Her husband, Jacob Gasala Kasongo, was born in Mukedi, also orphaned at an early age, and brought by missionaries to the Ndjoko Punda orphanage. There he became expert at raising chickens. The missionaries even used his name in a reader that contained a sentence, "Kasongo is feeding the chickens." Jacob was a model of good conduct for all the youth. The missionaries also trained him in carpentry, and put him through the mission's full education cycle. He became a teacher, founded a new congregation, and became assistant director of a collection of nine primary schools. In recognition of his accomplishments he was decorated with a bronze medal by the Belgian government in 1956.

Meanwhile, he also exercised his skills in carpentry. Curiously, the value of the articles Jacob made always rose. Along with his gift for raising chickens—he was a great purveyor of poultry and eggs to the missionaries—this activity brought him prosperity and reminded people of the Old Testament Jacob, son of Isaac and Rebecca and father of Joseph.

Jacob Gasala and Rebecca Gavunji also had a notable son, Samuel Kakesa, who became the first Congolese legal representative of the Mennonite Church in 1965.[2] The couple lived to see their son honored in this way. Rebecca Gavunji passed away in 1977, and Jacob Gasala died in 1984.

Jackson Beleji

2 See "An open Bible at rebel headquarters" (chapter 30).

9 ❧ Do Jesus people live in this village?

The fragile, pioneering work of the first Mennonite missionaries in Congo was guided by two critical decisions.

First, these early missionaries said that they would settle for nothing other than a single, intertribal Mennonite church. After all, in Christ walls of separation crumble and diverse people become brothers and sisters as they discover one another around the cross.

This decision reflected incredible faith, because the Belgian authorities, in authorizing various Protestant groups to work in the country, had allocated an area the size of Illinois to the Mennonites. This was the home territory of four major tribes, with another half-dozen or so overlapping ethnic groups around the edges, each with its own language, history, customs, and traditions.

Even more daunting was the bitter, bloody history between two of the major tribal groups, the Chokwe and the Pende. This conflict had its roots in an earlier era of Portuguese slave trade along the western coast of Central Africa. The Portuguese gave muskets and gunpowder to the Chokwe tribe and paid them for every person they captured and marched to the coast. The Pende tribe was a favorite target. Though this large-scale slave trade had stopped by the time the colonizing Belgians arrived, deep animosity remained between the two groups.

A second early decision was that Africans would become the primary, long-range evangelists of their own people. The missionaries realized that it was patently impossible for white-skinned folk from

North America alone to plant the intertribal Mennonite church of which they dreamed.

Thus a pattern of work quickly emerged. The missionaries worked toward the goal of evangelizing a first generation of believers and training them to become the primary witnesses to God's grace among their fellow villagers. Armed with three or four years of primary education plus study in a two-year Bible school, these African teacher-evangelists were placed in a widening radius around the early mission posts, where they settled in to open simple bush schools and to tell people about a man named Yesu.

The early going required grit and commitment in abundance. Typically the young African couples were not welcomed by village chiefs and their elders. What could the newcomers teach their boys that the villagers themselves could not teach them? Would the boys be better able to track antelope through the rolling grassland or set better snares for fish along the river's edge if they sat in the school and learned letters and numbers? Would they be better equipped to fashion fetishes to protect themselves from the dangerous spirits that prowled the darkness around their villages after sundown? Sometimes the newcomers came under the menace of witchcraft and even threats of death. But they persevered, couple after couple, and slowly over time the Lord honored their courageous faith. What celebration there was when they were able to baptize the first believers!

All of this was before the time of roads or any sort of mechanized transportation. Even bicycles were still rare. But travel by foot was nonetheless often necessary for villagers. This travel at times took people out of the area of their own ethnic group through that of adjoining tribes. Such travel was dangerous and not undertaken lightly. Strangers and "foreigners" making their way along the winding footpaths through the rolling savannah were easy targets. It was common for people to be robbed or even taken as slaves. There were persistent stories of people simply disappearing.

It was during this time that stories began circulating in African rural territory. Villagers were beginning to hear about "Jesus people" scattered here and there, even among the ethnic groups they feared and hated. The word was that they were people of kindness, generosity, and love— people to whom you could even entrust your life.

So when a traveler was approaching a village far from home at sundown, his first question was: "Do Jesus people live in this village?" If the answer was no, the traveler would often pass by, choosing to spend the night rolled up in his blanket under a bush somewhere. He was prepared to risk the dangers of a night among wild animals rather than stay in a village among people he feared.

But if "Jesus people" resided in that village, the traveler would ask to be directed to them, knowing that they would shelter and feed him regardless of his ethnic group or beliefs. He would be safe and the next morning would be sent on his way with a blessing.

Jim Bertsche

10 ❈ A well-ordered pastor

Some people are largely products of their environments, and others shape their own lives and their environments. Pierre Khelendende is one of those people who succeeded in imposing himself on his surroundings.

Pierre Khelendende was born in 1920 in a village near the Kandala mission station, to a peasant family that followed indigenous religion. Until his death, he never displayed the slightest regret about his origins. On the contrary, he was taken as a model by others of his generation despite his rural background. He followed a path similar to that of others who became Christians in that period. Many began as domestic servants, gardeners, or menial laborers. A missionary hired Khelendende as a cook when he was still a young boy. Khelendende was highly sought after for his construction skills, as well. He was baptized in 1940 and married Christine Ganji, a fellow Christian, in 1944. They would have four daughters.[1]

Khelendende diligently followed the missionary's biblical training and was consecrated by him. In this period, the mission needed teacher-evangelists. These lay people had as their main task the establishment of churches in villages distant from the mission station. Although he was only semiliterate, Pierre Khelendende went out to preach and teach the word of God. As the first black Christian teacher in the region, he had some influence. Despite his limited instruction,

photo—Christine Ganji and her husband, Pierre Khelendende

1 See "All I have to give is a daughter" (chapter 75).

Rev. Khelendende had a deep sense of responsibility and an exceptional spirituality. He captivated villagers by his moving and illuminating sermons, and many people converted to Christ as a result.

Khelendende became an example to others, especially for his instinct for what was beautiful and true. Propriety and elegance were his great preoccupations. "A pastor," he said, "ought to be well-ordered and disciplined in all things, because the God he serves is a God of order." As someone who loved justice and equality, he had much admiration for all the converts. Without any disdain toward anyone, Khelendende led a life of service and sharing. He spent his time visiting villages to spread the good news and shared the fruits of his evangelization with those who accompanied him, following the example of Jesus among his disciples.

Pastor Khelendende, like others in his position, made sacrifices and was convinced that God would bless from heaven the work of those who trusted him on earth and who worked firmly for him. He said that true happiness was clearly defined in the Beatitudes, Matthew 5:1–12.

Mennonite missionaries never fully resolved the logistical and material aspects of evangelists' lives in their formation of individuals. The missionaries did not want to encourage dependence or attract people into this ministry simply in the hope of a secure salary, so they did not put evangelists on the mission payroll. Instead, missionaries contributed to a congregation's treasury, as did other members, and congregations decided how to use these funds and whom to pay. But the missionaries' refusal to pay regular salaries to their recruits was a point of tension. Many of God's servants prominent in those early years worked under difficult circumstances. This was true of Pastor Khelendende. Having traveled great distances on foot in search of lost souls and then suffering the burdens of age, he died in poverty in 1988. Khelendende left good memories of his spirituality to the entire church and all those who had known him.

Vincent Ndandula

11 ❧ Daniel Khumbi, Christian nurse

The gospel brought by missionaries and evangelists transformed the lives of many people from small villages, making them see their lives in new ways. People who were transformed in turn brought these changes to other people in ways that over time grew to have great value and importance for the community. These believers often carried out this work of evangelism on their own without pay, in their free time, because of their love for God and for their neighbor. They strove for exemplary conduct, doing their best to treat others as they would want to be treated (Matthew 7:12). Daniel Khumbi is an example of this.

The brief story of the life of Daniel Khumbi begins with his primary schooling at the missionary station of Kamayala. If this boy from the village of Nambulu in the district of Kahemba had not enrolled at the primary school of Kamayala, his life would doubtless have passed unnoticed.

Daniel was drawn to medical work, so at the end of his primary schooling he went to work for Papa Joseph Kambembo, a nurse in the dispensary, as a room attendant. At that time, the missionaries cared for the health of both the Christian and the indigenous populations and provided medical training in each town in connection with a hospital supervised by one or two doctors. Daniel Khumbi received medical training under the supervision of the family doctor of Mukedi and became a nurse himself.

Daniel Khumbi showed great ability in his work. Because of this dedication and his exemplary conduct, he was invited to the hospital at Kajiji, situated approximately 100 kilometers from Kamayala. He turned down that request, however, because his parents preferred that their son work not too far from them. He married Ruth Makanga and they began their family life.

Little by little Daniel Khumbi initiated another ministry at the dispensary in Kamayala. After completing the medical tasks entrusted to him by Miss Bertha Miller, also called Mama Sadisa, Daniel Khumbi would meet with the patients as a chaplain. Seeing their suffering, he walked alongside them, sharing the pain of their illnesses.

It is necessary to explain at this point that most people, including many Christians, continued to be attached to traditional customs that were the foundation of African society. Daniel knew that in traditional society it is especially painful to watch a loved one suffer and die. With such passages as Job 14:13–15, he would comfort patients and their families by teaching them to know God and to know that God uses his omnipotence to give life even to the dead.

Many times the patients were also divided in their minds about the possible cause of their illness: it could be a natural illness resulting from a lack of hygienic conditions, or it could be the result of a curse caused by the anger of their dead ancestors. Transforming the dispensary into a parish, therefore, he brought people the good news of God's love for them and put them in touch with pastors. Many were baptized after their recovery.

Daniel Khumbi died in 1956, leaving Mama Ruth Makanga a widow with seven children.[1] The entire church has kept alive their memory of him not only as a gifted nurse but also as a loving Christian who extended to others a helping hand whenever possible.

Vincent Ndandula

1 See "Mama Ruth, mother of orphans" (chapter 12).

12 ⚜ Mama Ruth, mother of orphans

In many cultures, including many in Africa, women have been despised and undervalued, considered as objects of pleasure, cooks, unpaid babysitters, and incapable of rational speech. These erroneous attitudes have greatly restricted women's freedom and limited their accomplishments in certain areas.

Yet the traditional roles of homemaker and mother assigned to women in such cultures are tremendously important. Raising a child correctly requires love. It is in love that God has given to women the important assignment of accompanying men and teaching children. Proverbs 1:8–9 underlines the importance for children of teachings received from a mother as well as a father: "Listen, my son, to your father's instruction and do not forsake your mother's teaching. They are a garland to grace your head and a chain to adorn your neck" (NIV).

Mama Ruth Makanga played this role fully in the lives of young girls and boys in Kamayala. She was born in Nambulu around 1920, and her parents, who had certainly not gone to school, sent their daughter to the little school in Kamayala. People understood that you sent children to school not only so they would to learn to read and write but also so they would be transformed and transform the world in which they lived.

Ruth became the wife of Daniel Khumbi,[1] who was employed at the Kamayala dispensary. But he passed away in 1956, and Ruth became a widow. She had seven children.

After the death of her husband, Mama Ruth was employed by a missionary, Bertha Miller, to care for orphans. Ruth Makanga gave herself body and soul to these orphans as well as to her own children. Raising children is a task that belongs to parents or relatives. But to raise children whose parents one doesn't know can pose great challenges. Ruth Makanga demonstrated the full potential for love that a woman can carry within herself. She succeeded in raising her own children as well as those brought to her from the various villages touched by evangelization.

She also helped other women who wanted to bear children. Through prayer and by using medicinal plants that God placed in nature, Mama Ruth treated women who had fertility problems.

Many of those who benefited from her motherly warmth became leaders in the church or elsewhere and remained thankful. They report that while doing this work well, she considered that satisfaction and happiness are an illusion when they are sought for themselves. True satisfaction comes from a job well done.

Grounding her faith in Jesus Christ, Mama Ruth knew how to speak to men and to women, to build them up, to exhort them, and to console them. Blessed by the Eternal, this woman who knew how to share the joy and the suffering of children without parents spent more than eighty years on this earth. God called her to himself on June 1, 2000.

Vincent Ndandula

1 See "Daniel Khumbi, Christian nurse" (chapter 11).

13 ❧ Let's see if Archie is available

In 1930 there were four Mennonite mission posts in place in Congo—Ndjoko Punda, Kalamba, Nyanga, and Mukedi. But to the south between Djoko and Kalamba there was a rapidly growing government center named Tshikapa. At the confluence of two rivers, it was the locus of three powerful forces: the Belgian colonial government, a large Catholic mission, and the administrative headquarters of the Forminière diamond mining operation. Across the years Mennonite Christians had found their way to Tshikapa, looking for employment or training. Mennonite missionary Archie Graber made it his personal goal to establish a fifth mission post there.

Born into a rural Mennonite home near Stryker, Ohio, in 1901, Archie's early education was limited to eight years in a one-room school. A man of restless energy, he moved through an array of jobs, as an apprentice carpenter, a metalworker at Fisher Body in Detroit, a deckhand on a Great Lakes ore freighter, and (briefly) a ranch hand. At age twenty-four he drove a university professor to the West Coast. Over the long miles they got well acquainted. Learning that Archie had dropped out of school after the eighth grade, and sensing his potential, the professor strongly encouraged him to enroll in high school the following fall. He did so and took all the art classes he could. After recommitting his life to the Lord at a Bible conference at Winona Lake, Indiana, he enrolled at Moody Bible Institute in Chicago.

---

photo—Archie Graber (right) greeting friends

There Archie became aware of the nudging of God's Spirit toward mission service. In the process he also met Evelyn Oyer from Bloomington, Illinois, and discovered that she shared his sense of call. They were married in 1929, applied to Congo Inland Mission, and arrived in Congo in the spring of 1930. They were assigned to Ndjoko Punda, the pioneer post of the mission started just eighteen years earlier.

Archie quickly came to be known for (1) his passion for evangelism, linked with his love for the Africans around him, (2) his disregard for his personal safety in situations of potential danger, (3) his building skills, and (4) the artistic flair that he brought to everything he touched. For instance, at Ndjoko Punda he found a chapel that was no longer large enough for Sunday worship services. He remodeled and enlarged the building with a new exterior wall featuring lovely arched openings on the sides, and he added a bell tower over the entryway. Set among its palm trees, this place of worship was often photographed. He also made a communion table of mahogany buffed to a sheen with an ivory-inset Tshiluba scripture passage around the front edge: "This do in remembrance of me."

Archie had a place in mind for the new mission in Tshikapa. On trips to Tshikapa over the years he sought out a Baluba chief named Kalonda who had traditional rights over a gentle slope of land overlooking the Kasai River, the government offices, the airfield, and the Catholic mission in the distance. He explained to the chief the longstanding hope of the Mennonite mission to one day establish a presence on his land. He said that if that happened, the new mission post would be named Kalonda in the chief's honor. The chief signaled his agreement—indeed, his eagerness—to grant this permission.

In early 1945 the Grabers returned to the States for a furlough, but they were living under a cloud. Evelyn, who was musically gifted, had plunged into the life of the African church, translating hymns into Tshiluba and frequently singing with Congolese students during worship services. But she was not well. Despite all medical intervention, she died in 1946. Archie couldn't think of returning to Congo without her. There followed a time of deep sorrow and a pause in his missionary life.

Meanwhile in Congo, missionaries were making repeated requests for permission to occupy ground at Tshikapa and were being rebuffed on all fronts. It was only after the conclusion of World

War II that the barricades were finally breached. Following the Allied victory, a political upheaval in Belgium threw the ruling Catholic party out of power. The new regime immediately leveled the playing field for Christian missions in Congo, offering generous subsidies for Protestant and Catholic missions alike for medical and educational work that met their standards. Although legally the door was now open, entrenched Belgian personnel in Congo still resisted. It was at that point that an appeal was made in Leopoldville, the capital, via the intervention of the Protestant Council of Congo office of the city.

Though still grieving when he heard this news, Archie packed his bags and returned to Ndjoko Punda, where he immediately went to work directing the construction of a large school building to house a new teacher-training program, which the mission was able to offer because of new government help. As he worked he kept in touch with the missionary field chairman via shortwave radio, repeatedly asking, "Have the papers come yet?"

When they finally arrived, Archie threw a few housekeeping items into his pickup and headed south for Tshikapa. He went straight to Chief Kalonda's village and shared the good news. With long bamboo poles topped with white rags they made their way back and forth across the land, the chief jabbing the poles into the soil here and there, marking the territory. Meanwhile Archie's mind was racing. The chapel will be over there, a clinic to this side, a primary school yonder, missionary residences down there overlooking the river, and a Bible school for the entire mission off to the left. In time, all his dreams came true.

The Africans remember Archie best as a preacher. His grasp of the Tshiluba language was never perfect. The intricate agreement patterns between nouns, verbs, and adjectives, so typical of Bantu languages, sometimes escaped him. But once he was on the platform and launched into his message, he was a powerful communicator. He spent little time behind the pulpit but instead roamed the platform. Sometimes he would illustrate his message by sketching scenes with colored chalk on a small blackboard. His love for the people before him registered clearly with them. Many Africans across the years responded to his passionate appeals to place their faith and trust in Jesus. It was for a good reason that in his first term at Ndjoko Punda the Africans named him Muambi Lutonga, the young preacher.

Among the single missionary women on the mission team was Irma Beitler from Berne, Indiana, a competent nurse with a quick smile and upbeat personality. During lonely evenings on the compound in the second phase of his missionary career, Archie found himself wondering if she might consider a proposal of marriage. Shyly communicating his secret hopes, he was delighted to discover that he was not rebuffed. They were married in the spring of 1951. Irma was his constant companion through the tumultuous years that were to follow.

The next jobs Archie took on were two projects related to education. A growing team had to make arrangements to educate missionary children. The mission secured a parcel of land in Leopoldville and raised funds to build a hostel. The committee asked whether Archie was available. Challenged by the opportunity, he accepted. In time a lovely two-story building rose among the tropical trees and flowering shrubs of the plot, a home away from home for dozens of missionary kids through their primary and high school years.

Africa Inter-Mennonite Mission (as Congo Inland Mission is now called) decided to participate with other missions in establishing a pastor training program in the capital. This enormous building project included office space, classrooms, dorms for students, a chapel, storage, and more. One of the missions offered a builder, and the project began. But progress was slow, work teams were inefficient, and materials were not always at hand when needed. The original deadline for moving in would not be met. In the midst of mounting dissatisfaction, someone asked if that Mennonite builder was available. Archie didn't need a second invitation. Organizing work teams and setting daily goals for them to finish, he named his own date for completion. Suddenly buildings started to rise, and participating missions began to plan the arrival of their students. Celebration abounded.

But nothing would test Archie's visionary leadership like the call that came in late 1960 to come to the aid of refugees fleeing the post-independence tribal wars.[1]

Jim Bertsche

1 Archie's story is continued in Part III. See "Feeding the refugees of South Kasai" (chapter 39).

14 ꕥ Gladys Fox, unlikely donor

I found the sheets of 5" x 8" tablet paper in an "F" folder tagged "miscellaneous" in the Africa Inter-Mennonite Mission archives. The upcoming centennial celebration of Congo Inland Mission had prompted us to comb through these archives, which are in the custody of the Illinois Historical and Genealogical Society near Metamora, Illinois.

Tucked among routine housekeeping materials, which we sorted and threw away, were these one-page notes, written in pencil. They were dated in the 1930s and 1940s and addressed to Rev. C. E. Rediger, secretary-treasurer of Congo Inland Mission. Not all the notes had a return address, but those that did were marked simply "Flanagan, Illinois."

In note after note, the message was essentially the same: "Enclosed find my check in the amount of $300"—or $200 or $400. There would sometimes be a brief suggestion for how to use it in Congo—for a boy's dormitory at such and such a station, roofing on a girl's school at another station, or Christian literature somewhere else. Now and again a line would be added: "Please do not attach my name to the gift."

At the bottom of each note was the same penciled name: Gladys Fox.

Two things astonished me. First was the size of the gifts. Times were hard in rural America in the 1930s and 1940s. Even a twenty-

photo—Gladys Fox

dollar gift to Congo Inland Mission during those decades was considered generous. But here came these periodic checks, each made out for hundreds of dollars!

Even more surprising was that they came from Gladys Fox. I knew Gladys well when I was a schoolboy. We both attended Salem Mennonite Church, located between Gridley and Flanagan, Illinois.

Gladys had come from Kansas in response to the advertised need for help at the nearby Salem Children's Home. Serving at the home as matron of small boys, she received board and room and a stipend for her services. But my boyhood impression was that this tall, large-boned woman with an awkward, swinging stride did not have much money.

Gladys seemed to have two or three summer dresses and two or three winter ones. She always wore the same no-nonsense black shoes. She wore her hair in long braids wrapped around her head, covering them with a knitted cap in winter. She seemed shy, rarely initiating conversation. She clearly was not a woman who sought attention. Above all, one had the sense that whether because she wanted to or needed to, she pinched her pennies.

But here were those sheets torn from a tablet with the penciled notes, dating back to the era of economic depression and then war in our country, recording gifts to Congo Inland Mission of many hundreds of dollars! How was that possible?

Finally, I found the note that explained everything.

"Dear Mr. Rediger, I have recently received an inheritance from my mother. I have been praying about how to use it. The Lord is leading me to give it to help support missionary work in the Congo. Please keep me informed about needs there. Gladys."

I read and reread that note as I summoned up my boyhood memories of the Gladys I knew. Even as she limited herself to a frugal wardrobe and lived a simple life, she was quietly sending checks to Congo Inland Mission and asking to remain anonymous. In one of those notes she said, "My family would not understand."

At centennial time, we are coming to realize more and more that across the years God has been at work on both sides of the ocean. God's Spirit was stirring the hearts of simple rural people in North America to volunteer for missionary service. God was also at work convicting people in the pews of Mennonite congregations to pray and to give generously, even sacrificially, so a new inter-Mennonite presence and witness in the heart of Africa could grow. Indeed CIM/AIMM has been God's doing all along. Thank you, Lord.

Jim Bertsche

15 ꕥ He sold corn at ten cents a bushel to raise boat fare

In a rural Mennonite church in central Illinois in the fall of 1932, a young couple shared their dream of missionary service in Congo. The couple was Russell and Helen Yoder Schnell. The church was the North Danvers Mennonite Church, the congregation that twenty years earlier had sent Lawrence and Rose Boehning Haigh as two of the first three pioneering missionaries of Congo Inland Mission (CIM).

The Schnells had been accepted by this mission. They had their outfit gathered and packed. All that stood between them and their departure was the last hundred dollars needed for their boat fare from New York City to Matadi, the seaport of Congo.

In the congregation that Sunday sat Ali and Anna Weidinger Stahly, a farming couple. It was their custom to invite visiting missionaries to their home for Sunday dinner. In that informal setting the Schnells were able to give much more detail about their plans and needs than had been possible during the morning service. Also seated at the table were two sons, Ali Jr. and Maurice, who were quietly listening to the flow of conversation around the table.

It was in the depths of the great depression. Money was scarce. Some farmers around the Stahlys were in danger of losing their farms because they could not meet their mortgage payments to local

photo—Ali Stahly as a young man

banks. As a matter of fact, Ali Sr. had been named to a federal commission that was negotiating between area farmers and their banks, trying to find ways for the farmers to keep their land.

But Ali carried an even greater concern for the newly launched Mennonite mission venture in the distant Congo. He went to bed that night with the stark realization that all that stood between this young couple and their departure for the land of their calling was one hundred dollars. At some point during the night he made a decision.

The next morning he instructed his oldest son, Ali Jr., to hitch a team of horses to a box wagon and begin hauling ear corn from his bins to the local elevator. He was to continue hauling until he had racked up a credit of a hundred dollars. The price for corn was ten cents a bushel. In other words, the Stahlys sold 1,000 bushels!

A check was forthwith sent to the Schnells. Before year's end they arrived in Congo and were assigned to the CIM mission post at Ndjoko Punda, the place where the first trio of pioneers had set foot twenty years earlier.

All of this was not lost on the younger Stahly son, Maurice. Though he did not fully comprehend what was happening, one thing was clear to him: missionary work in distant Africa was extremely important to his parents. Memories of that ten-cent-a-bushel corn stayed with Maurice throughout his life.

Graduating from high school in 1939, he secured employment in an area Caterpillar plant. Three years later he married Opal Bostic and that same year was drafted. Applying for Civilian Public Service, he spent three years as an orderly in a hospital in Harrisburg, Pennsylvania. Upon completing his service, he and Opal wondered what was next for them. Reflecting on that time, Maurice later commented: "We felt God saying to us, 'Some I send out. Others I call to stay at home and support the work of the kingdom.'"[1]

Maurice eventually became a trucker, then acquired his own trucking fleet. But as his business flourished, he continued learning about God's ways. Reflecting on that era, he observes: "I started out by saying, 'God, I want to use you in my business.' But I found out God says, 'It's my business and I want to use you.' It took me almost

---

1 Steve Bowers, "What We Share with Teaspoons," *Sharing*, Winter 1992.

20 years to figure that out. Too often, we want to use God instead of Him using us.'"[2]

Along the way Maurice became involved with a variety of denominational boards and committees as well as the boards of Mennonite Mutual Aid, Mennonite Foundation, and Mennonite Economic Development Associates.

But no commitment or involvement has been more enduring than his relationship with Congo Inland Mission/Africa Inter-Mennonite Mission. He served as a board member from 1956 to 1975. It was during that time that he made an extensive trip to Congo with fellow board members. To this day, framed photographs of the trip grace the walls of his office. As he kept current with AIMM news, gifts for the work continued to find their way to the AIMM office in Goshen, Indiana, from a rural Mennonite church in central Illinois.

When told the vision of this centennial story project, Maurice Stahly was the first to write a large check to support it. He said the contribution was a memorial to his father. Maurice passed away in April 2012 as the project was reaching its final stages.

All of us who have learned about Maurice Stahly's boyhood in the home of a farmer father with a deep commitment to God's work are grateful for the shared memory of that hundred dollars raised by selling ear corn at ten cents a bushel.

Jim Bertsche

---

2 Ibid.

16 ⚜ Joseph Kibuza, chaplain

Most of the people of the village on the outskirts of Mukedi were indifferent to the message of the first white missionaries who came to them in 1923. White people were entitled to their God, but village people were busy trying to cope with their own belief system. They too believed in a creating God but one who had withdrawn long ago and cared nothing about them. They were left to deal with the daily threat of evil spirits and the constant fear of witchcraft and death.

But with time the Lord honored the persistent witness of those first missionaries, and a few people began to ask questions. As the Spirit worked, a small handful of adults experienced the joy of peace that came from accepting Jesus into their hearts. Among them was a man named Kibuza. In his village he was known as one who had been deeply immersed in sorcery, but when he accepted Christ as his Savior, the change in his life was dramatic.

By that time the missionaries had opened a school. To Kibuza's deep regret, he was too old to enroll, but every time there was any sort of activity in the little grass chapel on the station, he was there, soaking it all up. He began to memorize the hymns that were sung. Several of his nephews were enrolled in the mission school and were beginning to read and write. Sometimes they brought home scraps of paper on which they'd written words of God in Gipende, their language. Kibuza would call them to his home after school, seat them,

photo—Joseph Kibuza

and ask that they slowly read the passages again and again. Before long, Kibuza was quoting Bible passages. He became a member of one of the earliest baptismal groups. Upon being baptized and taken into the Mukedi church, he chose the name Joseph.

Meanwhile, new medical work at Mukedi, led by Merle and Dorothy Schwartz,[1] was growing by leaps and bounds. Expectant mothers and people who were sick or injured were coming from surrounding villages in increasing numbers. The Schwartzes and their small Congolese staff had their hands full. They wanted to use this opportunity for witness to the hundreds who were coming for help. They needed a hospital chaplain, but who was available? When they shared their need with the local church council, a suggestion quickly followed: "What about Joseph Kibuza? He's had no schooling but he knows our hymns, he's memorized a lot of scripture, and above all else, he loves the Lord."

So Joseph, a man who couldn't write his own name, was added to the Mukedi medical staff. A neat little pole-and-thatch chapel was built adjacent to the hospital. Each morning, bright and early, Kibuza was there to greet people and invite them into the little chapel, where he would sing a few hymns, quote a passage of scripture—all from memory—and then tell his fellow villagers about Jesus. They were illiterate, just as he was, and lived in constant fear of death, just as he once had. His enthusiasm was infectious.

Joseph Kibuza was also busy in his home village of Mukedi next door to the mission station. Over time he had led a small group of his peers to a life-changing faith in Christ. Kibuza was delighted, but at the same time he was becoming aware of a problem. He only knew so many passages of scripture. He and the other believers wanted to learn more.

He paid me a visit and made a request. If he and his village fellow believers would come to the station chapel an hour early each Sunday morning, would I come and feed them with the word of God? He pointed out that he and his friends always came to church but sometimes didn't understand everything they heard, and there was no chance to ask questions. Thus was born a weekly routine. Each Sunday morning, fifteen minutes before the pre-service meeting time, there would be a reminder knock at my back door. A smiling Joseph would announce: "Your children are waiting for you!"

---

1 See "The unsinkable Schwartzes" (chapter 38).

I came to treasure the hours with these believers. On one occasion I reflected with the group on John 14:1–4: "Do not let your hearts be troubled. . . . I go to prepare a place for you." Right in front of me was seated a toothless granny, dressed in a sun-bleached blouse and frayed wraparound skirt. Her face was a map of wrinkles. Her flip-flops gave full view of toenails worn to buttons by years of encounters with rocks and roots on numberless treks along winding footpaths to her fields. Shaking her calloused hand was like rubbing the side of a leather briefcase. I doubt that she had ever been as much as fifty miles from her village.

As I taught, the old woman's eyes never left my face. Then, on an impulse, I addressed a question to her: "*Khakha* [Grandmother], when your days on this earth are finished, where will you go?" Without an instant's hesitation and without a word, she smiled and pointed a finger skyward.

And down at the end of the church bench sat Joseph Kibuza, an expression of sheer delight on his face.

Jim Bertsche

17 ⁂ David Masheke, Lele evangelist and teacher

A descendant of the Lele tribe, David Masheke was born at Ndimbu in the sector of Basonga in 1914. Around 1920, Masheke was required in spite of himself to leave his mother to begin his elementary school education. Young children like David often couldn't understand why they were being shut up in a room or forced to sit under a tree under the authority of a teacher instead of being allowed to go and play. But it was for their own good and that of the whole village. After a few years of schooling, they were usually happy to stay in school.

Still, in the regions like the one in which he was born, nature offered many opportunities to earn a living through agricultural production and hunting. The temptation was great to stay in the village and enjoy the products of nature rather than go to school.

But young David Masheke was happy to go through elementary school, then study for two more years at the evangelical school at Ndjoko Punda. At the end of the intensive training, he was hired by the mission as a secretary. He continued in this role for four years, from 1943 to 1947. Having acquired some experience in this work, he became a better typist and was much appreciated by the missionaries. In 1943 he married Mboyo Mashosho; they would have eight children.

At the end of 1947 he ceased working as a secretary-typist and gave himself over completely to the work of evangelization, traveling from one village to another. It was a difficult pilgrimage, but it allowed the extension of the Mennonite mission among the Lele people. He is considered one of the pioneers who laid the first stone in the construction of the Banga mission. But David Masheke also played an important role in the awakening of the Lele people through his work.

He had a vision: to bring his people to recognize not only the marvels that nature offered but also the omnipotent God, creator of all things, who had put all things at the disposal of his people because of his great love for them. Even while preaching the good news of salvation, he encouraged young people to pursue an education for the well-being of the church and of the region.

Around 1958, teacher-evangelist David Masheke caught leprosy, an illness that is difficult to treat and that slowly eats away at the sufferer. Seven years later, he went to meet the Lord. Despite the brevity of his life, he had the honor of having opened the way to schooling and to salvation for many people from his community.

Vincent Ndandula

18 ⚘Joseph the Ringer

The missionaries first encountered him by the side of his uncle, the traditional chief at Holesa, a border village near Angola. He probably actually came from Angola. In these border villages, the populations often carry a double identity, because the tribal territories do not follow national boundaries. People may identify themselves as Congolese or Angolan, depending on the circumstances. In any case, Joseph Munange never spoke about his birth or his parents, and he spent his life in Congo, where he had a family into which he was well integrated.

Because certain populations were hostile toward outside influences, the missionaries always looked for means of negotiation to allow them to do their work in peace. Often it was from the entourage of the chief that men were chosen to serve as interpreters or project managers. Munange was one of the persons designated by the village chief to lend a hand to the missionaries. They asked the chief for authorization to take him to Kalamba Mukenge to receive biblical training there for the benefit of his family and all the population. The chief agreed to this.

After his biblical training, Munange, now called Joseph, was immediately assigned as teacher-evangelist of Tshisaka. Later he would serve other villages. Joseph had a particular passion for morning prayer. Each day he woke up early to ring the bell for worship. In one village he served, they called him Joseph the Ringer.

---

photo—Joseph Munange

Joseph Munange dedicated himself to the evangelism of his Chokwe brothers and sisters in the territory situated between the Kasai and Kwilu rivers and shared his vision with Pastor Noel Kahuku in that region. A present-day pastor affirms that Joseph had a strong conviction of the power of God over the forces of evil. Knowing perfectly well that Chokwe society often resorts to practices involving fetishes and sorcery, he always used to say, "Christianity is able to be victorious over the spirits and the traditional spiritual forces."

Joseph Munange was aware of his limited formal education. In the face of the demands for developing the church in a new context, he sent rising youth to study in order to ensure that there would be successors for his work in the future. A number of these individuals are leaders today.

Before his death in 2002, he sought to leave his church one great accomplishment. He mobilized the churches in the area to become self-governing. He succeeded in creating a new church district with its headquarters in Ngombe.

At his death, no one spoke about his Angolan origins. The church praised the Lord for having used this man through whom many souls found the way to eternal salvation.

Vincent Ndandula

19 ⁂ Papa Daniel, a nurse in service to all

A first-generation Christian born in 1918, Daniel Kidinda was the eldest of a family of five children. Later he would take an older brother's responsibility for his younger siblings, but Papa Daniel would serve many others besides his immediate family.

He was an exemplary child by all accounts: modest, sociable, and kind. He completed five years of primary education at the Mennonite mission of Mukedi, followed by two years of evangelical studies. This certificate enabled him to be accepted as a student nurse at the Mukedi hospital. He then added two years of nursing courses. His nursing studies concluded with a board examination, which he passed, obtaining a certificate in nursing science. After being truly converted to God, he followed religious instruction and was baptized at Mukedi in 1937.

Daniel Kidinda married Henriette Khajia, and they had two children before she passed away. He married Mama Denise Foto in 1947 and had ten children with her.

He rendered many services to the population. First he served as a nurse at several places, ending up at the Mukedi hospital. He believed that nothing is impossible with God and that all healing comes from God, despite the existence of medicines. His manner of care gave his patients total confidence in him. They preferred to be treated by him rather than by others, because of his knowledge, competence, and experience.

To practice his faith, Daniel never began work without telling the good news to his patients. Because of his teachings of the word of God, some of these patients came to faith.

The esteem of the local population propelled him to membership on the council working with the chief administering the Lozo sector. At this level he came to judge people with justice. After having exercised the functions of sector counselor, he went to work for himself, opening his own private clinic.

In his clinic he cared for the sick with confidence without staking too much on money matters. He treated patients even if they didn't have money, hoping they would pay their bills when they could. What was important for him was to save people first and ask for payment later.

The family of Daniel Kidinda has been blessed. After the death of his first wife, Daniel Kidinda and his second wife did their best in bringing up the two motherless children as well as their ten. His children are employed in various capacities. One of his children is in France.

He was a man who brought others together, a kind man, social and obliging. Papa Daniel Kidinda, eldest of his family, carefully nurtured his younger sisters and brothers. He showered affection and esteem on the youngest of the family, Philidor Mukedi, who graduated from teachers college and is currently director of one of the schools of the denomination and an elder as well.

The irreproachable merits of Papa Daniel Kidinda and his good works made him a man of great worth. He passed away in 1982, leaving behind in the social sector a private health center.

Jackson Beleji

20 ❧ Moise Musenvu, international evangelist

The man with the shaggy beard went about the countryside, carrying his raffia bag containing several tattered Sunday school posters. His favorite was one with images of the human heart. He was like the local clown that you often see in African villages. Many people called him crazy.

But Moise Musenvu was not crazy. If you asked him who he was, he would respond with a smile, "I am an international evangelist." And he was. He was an evangelist without borders, a responsible human being who lived on what he earned.

Moise Musenvu was born around 1915 in a village a few kilometers from the Mukedi mission station. Simple curiosity drew him, like other children, to watch what the white-skinned people were doing in the neighboring village. At first these white people were considered ghosts and called *mindele.* Literally that means "comes from far away or from the beyond."

Hired initially to haul water and then to break stones for the construction of the church, the boy was introduced to his first notions of reading and mathematics at the Mukedi station. After two or three years in elementary school, he spent several months at the Bible school organized to train teacher-evangelists. Quickly he astonished the missionaries by his memorization of Bible verses and

photo—Moise Musenvu

his eloquence in reciting them. He soon took responsibility for educating small children.

Moise was baptized and then married Esther. Together they would have six children, three girls and three boys. Two of the girls had severe birth defects.

In that era the American Mennonite missionaries had trouble expressing themselves in French, although they were fluent in the dialects of the tribes they evangelized. Their difficulties influenced the speech of their first pupils, including Moise. This man translated his thoughts literally into French without reference to grammatical correctness or proper tense. He might say, for example, "Christians not talk lie."

Moise Musenvu, a man of action and initiative, was a great hog farmer. After every butchering, he distributed part of the meat to little children and the needy. His family often reproached him for his great generosity to others while he neglected his own offspring, but he never showed any regret for that.

It was never enough for Moise to be a farmer. He set his sights on the ideal expressed by Christ in Matthew 28:18–20, "Go and make of all the earth my disciples." Moise became an evangelist to the world that he knew, disregarding the limits of religious faiths and denominations. Humble, peaceful, smiling, comical Moise would go to preach, in his poor French, to Catholics, Kimbanguists (an indigenous church), Muslims, and Protestants, all mixed together. With no means of transport, this spiritual vagabond covered great distances on foot. His trademark was the posters he carried with images of the human heart, symbol of the conversion of souls to eternal salvation.

Once he surprised the late President Mobutu with his mobility. The president, who was traveling by airplane, saw Moise in a parade in Gungu, two days later in Kikwit, and a third time at Bandundu. He did not understand how this man could be following him around.

Perhaps the most important and surprising thing about Moise was his absolute fearlessness and simplicity. He would show up in military camps, in prisons, in stadiums—everywhere. When he was asked who he was, he would cheerfully announce, "I am an international evangelist."

Moise played the *nguaya,* a traditional instrument, and through these local songs he brought traditional folklore into his spirituality. His local village church did not approve of this approach, and he was not accepted there—but Mennonites were not well established in the cities at that time. This man greatly influenced the planting of Mennonite congregations in towns such as Gungu and Kahemba and in the city of Kikwit.

Moise hoped to get a jeep, which would have allowed him to cover all the Democratic Republic of Congo and neighboring countries as a true international evangelist. But he died in 1987, before that dream could be realized. He is still remembered fondly, especially by women and by children, now grown, who knew him.

Vincent Ndandula

21 ⚘ Elie Kahanga, bachelor pastor

One of Congo's early Mennonite pastors brought a consistent message of the need for Christian unity. Perhaps it was because he was atypical in so many ways: member of a minority tribe, crippled, originating from another denomination, and—most unusual of all in this society—single all his life.

Elie Kahanga was born in 1907 not far from the Baptist mission in Vanga. A member of the Mbala tribe, he left his natal village when he was sixteen to live at the mission. The mission stations attracted many people, because they were the key to changing the lives of those who joined them. Elie studied four years and became a teacher-evangelist. The Baptist missionaries took note of his competence, trusted him, and used him as an interpreter and guide for the white people who arrived in the region for the first time.

At the end of 1929, he was asked to serve as a guide for a family that was traveling from Vanga to Kamayala, site of a Mennonite mission. Elie Kahanga chose to stay with them, and so began a pilgrimage that would take him definitively away from his birthplace.

At Kamayala, Elie didn't hesitate to use his talents as a devout teacher-evangelist. He spent several years teaching reading and writing the gospel to young people at the Kamayala station. His success in evangelization led to his ordination as a pastor, a role in which he served until his death.

Rev. Elie Kahanga with his bicycle

In 1958, Congo Inland Mission decided to install pastors permanently in outlying areas, in order to better teach people and convert them. However, many pastors were reluctant to leave the mission station. Pastor Elie Kahanga was the first to submit and go to live in a substation, where he served the rest of his life. With the support of missionaries, he solicited subsidies from the state and built a permanent school building with five classrooms.

Even today in Congo it is almost unheard of for a man to pass his entire life unmarried, but this man of God did so. The story is that Pastor Elie was engaged to marry a woman who fell passionately in love with another man. Severely disappointed, Elie decided to live alone, fearing that any woman might prove as unfaithful as she. This was a serious, risky decision, but he remained true to it. The testimonies about his life indicate that he nevertheless led an exemplary life. Few people today could match him.

Another difficult event could have further discouraged him but seemed to have no adverse effect. On one of his evangelistic tours by bicycle, he was pedaling along, singing in Chokwe, "I am shaken by sadness at the death of Christ," when he lost control and crashed in the ditch. He ended up with a twisted ankle that handicapped him for the rest of his life. He categorized all of his difficulties as Satan's temptations to turn him away from the way of salvation.

His life conveyed several important lessons. In his messages to Christians, Pastor Elie Kahanga never ceased to say that the road to eternal life is long and full of obstacles. But in order to get there we must, in fraternity, hospitality, and sociability, witness to our solidarity around the cross of Jesus Christ.

Also, like the Apostle Paul, who lived as a Greek among the Greeks, Pastor Kahanga showed that in Jesus Christ there are no tribal barriers. Coming from Mbala origins, he lived among the Lunda and Chokwe without any complexes. Nor could anyone imagine that he had come from another denomination. Suffering criticism and scorn because he was without wife and children, he managed to rise above it and loyally execute his calling.

Pastor Kahanga tried to get his church to engage in agriculture and animal husbandry for the sake of economic development, but that idea wasn't well understood at the time. Nevertheless, when he passed away in the 1990s, he left everything that belonged to him to the church.

Vincent Ndandula

22 ⚜ Paul Djoko, Christian elder and chief

Elder Paul Djoko's life shows how the Christianity of the missionaries was woven into a culture that was both traditionally African and dominated by colonialism.

In theory, the colonial authorities required all children to learn to read and write, but to provide the schools they depended on the missions—initially the Catholic missions and later the Protestant ones as well. If village authorities were caught resisting the invitation to send their children to a village school, they could be punished.[1] In that era of the whip, no one was inclined to accept public flogging and the heavy fines imposed for serious infringement of the law.

It was in this context that studies began for Djoko, who was born in 1910 of parents who were members of the Pende tribe from the territory of Tshikapa. Because he was attending a mission school, being a good student also meant memorizing a certain number of Bible verses. Upon finishing studies, one obtained a certificate and then was expected to convert to Christianity. In 1930, Djoko was a man doubly crowned. He had just completed his studies, and he had just been baptized.

Professional life opened before him, with all its suffering, obstacles, and responsibilities. The Bible declares in Genesis 2:18, "It is not good for the man to be alone; I will make for him a helper like

1 See "A Mennonite evangelist tied to a corpse" (chapter 1).

him." And so Paul married Thérèse in 1932. Together they had six children. For a woman in African society, birth is experienced as a happy event, because the child increases the power of the lineage. To have many children is a great blessing; to have none is a misery.

Paul was employed as a teacher-evangelist from 1932 to 1934. Then he decided to leave that role and become chief of his village as well as a judge in the traditional court of his sector. Both roles were strongly tied to ancestral traditions.

As paradoxical as it may seem, he showed a great attachment to Christian faith, participating actively in the life of his local church. He was ordained deacon in 1965 and elected to serve as an evangelist by the district. Often ignoring his role as village chief, he traveled up and down to several villages to evangelize people there with the good news of salvation, to create prayer cells, and to encourage the population to build churches and schools in the areas under his ministry.

Weakened by diabetes, he died on August 28, 2003. His local church, of which he was a full member, organized a funeral worthy of a Christian, because in all of his life—including the exercise of his traditional role—he was humble and God-fearing, his behavior above reproach.

Vincent Ndandula

23 ❧ Two leaders in Wongo territory

In their evangelistic work, the missionaries encountered great difficulties in certain territories that were entrenched in indigenous spiritual and magical practices. In such territories, certain individuals were key to opening these groups to the gospel. André Yumbu and Jérémie Ndjare served as such leaders among their people, the Wongo, one of the smaller tribes in the Kwilu district of Bandundu Province. This was in the general territory served by the Mukedi mission.

André Yumbu was born in 1910. In his youth, Yumbu accompanied his father on big game hunts and smaller hunts, during which he tended traps in the Loange River. Although his parents followed indigenous religion, they believed in God, "Zambi wa Mpungu." This is what prompted André's father to tell him about the arrival of white missionaries in Mukedi, and in time to send the boy to the mission to study.

André went through primary school there and was baptized at the same mission in 1937. He married and had ten children. He was hired as a teacher at the mission station that had received him and opened his horizons. Shortly thereafter he was employed as a supervisor of the Wongo schools.

As the premier intellectual in Wongo country, he was named chief of the Kilembe sector, a government position, at independence. Because of his skills, he served in this capacity from 1960 to 1972. He

---

photos—Jérémie Ndjare (left); André Yumbu (right)

was loved by all of his people for his patience, spirit, and sense of responsibility. This counselor and honest educator also proved to be dedicated to the welfare of other people outside his tribe.

Just as he was appreciated for his administrative skills, Yumbu was also recognized by the church for his irreproachable conduct, competence, and sense of responsibility. The Mennonite Church of Congo (CMCo) put him in charge of planting churches in Wongo territory. The means he used to do this were no more or less than the preaching of the message of salvation to indigenous peoples. Aside from believing in a supreme being, the Wongo were completely ignorant of the gospel. It was Yumbu who brought them the good news. His exceptional courage aided the success of his mission.

As André Yumbu was rising as an administrator and church leader, Jérémie Ndjare, another Wongo tribe member, was beginning three years of study at the Kalonda Bible Institute. He had hardly finished in 1963 when he was ordained a pastor in response to the burgeoning interest in the gospel in Wongo territory. For ten years he devoted himself to converting souls among his tribe and others as well. He then returned to his birthplace, Banga, and assumed an administrative leadership position in the church.

Ndjare was devoted to his ministry and saw the need to further his education to better meet the exigencies of evangelization in the rapidly changing environment of post-independence. He went to Kinshasa for studies that ended in 1980, and then returned to his district. His church elected him head of the Kalonda district from 1982 to 1985. At the end of his term, in all simplicity and humility he took on the role of chaplain at Tshikapa general hospital and worked there until 1997. At an advanced age he was called on to head yet another church district of the CMCo.

Christians sought out and appreciated Ndjare for his works and his character as a peacemaker. During this time conflict arose over the succession to leadership of the community. But Pastor Ndjare fought with all his strength to maintain unity in the community torn apart by tribal differences.

He never stopped preaching that Jesus Christ, who is head of the church, was not attached to a single tribe. If Jesus had been attached to a tribe, he pointed out, we would not be in his service today. Taking himself as an example of membership in a minority tribe, his message was that in Jesus Christ tribe, ethnicity, and other differences no longer have meaning.

Through their evangelization and church planting, André Yumbu and Jérémie Ndjare brought the number of church districts in the region to six. Currently the CMCo is widespread among the Wongo. Among these Mennonites are evangelists, deacons, elders, and pastors whose mission is to propagate the gospel of Jesus Christ. These people cannot speak of the development of their church without remembering these two leaders and examples.

Jackson Beleji and Vincent Ndandula

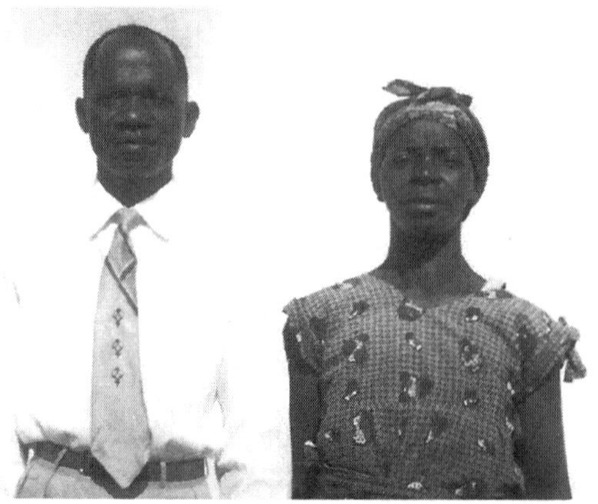

24 ❧ A small man of giant wisdom

In 1926, a boy named Wayindama was born in the territory of Kahemba. At that time, many areas were not yet evangelized. The villagers still lived under the weight of their customs and traditions. The missionaries were still in the phase of exploration and initial contact for the planting of Christianity.

The young Wayindama began his primary education at age nine, was baptized in 1940, and took the name Emmanuel. He finished his basic education in 1941 at Kamayala. Very gifted, this man of small stature, slim but wise, was appointed teacher in Mutalawanga, then in Kamayala. He had participated in a competition to select the best candidates, and was selected as one of them. Married to Eunice Kamena, he continued his studies at the Kalonda Bible Institute, where he later became a professor.

In 1962, unrest rocked the country. Xenophobia was everywhere. No one wanted to be under the supervision of foreigners. The various tribal wars in the region of the Kasai created a gulf between the Baluba, Pende, Lulua, and Chokwe. In this context, Wayindama left the Kasai for Kandala, where the Bible institute was transferred. But things deteriorated quickly because of the fighting that broke out in the region.[1] Rev. Emmanuel Wayindama was forced to go back to his native Kamayala.

Emmanuel Wayindama with his wife Eunice Kamena

1 For more about Wayindama's role at this time, see "That's all you can do to me" (chapter 26).

The first thing to remember is that this man was the first pastor in the territory of Kahemba with extensive biblical training. Many had become pastors with limited biblical training, on the basis of the missionaries' esteem and recommendation. His solid training contributed greatly to the growth of his strong and peaceful personality.

The second thing to remember was his contribution to translating the Bible into local languages. He was part of the team for translating the Chokwe Bible. He believed that preaching in the local trade language was not enough; Christians needed to be given opportunity to read the Bible in their native tribal tongue, so they could meditate on the word of God. A translation in their own language would constitute an important factor in the strengthening and deepening of Christianity. According to him, Christianity had to become something that belonged to each community. It should not be a foreign object. On the contrary, it had to take root in the culture, morals, and ideas of the people who received it.

Responding to the call of the Lord in going anywhere the church needed him, he was a man open to others. His open-mindedness permitted him to put himself completely at the service of his fellows. Testimonies from the local church portray him as the pioneer of the orientation course at the missionary station in Kandala. He was also the source of inspiration for many young leaders.

But the church, though it preached the gospel, the truth, did not pay much attention to the material needs of its servants, at least not to those of its black servants who put themselves at its disposal. These men and woman who responded to the call of Christ did so at the peril of their health, because they lacked transportation. Covering large distances on bicycle or on foot, Rev. Wayindama was employed over and over to settle and arbitrate conflicts, belonging as he did to the class of the wise.

In spite of these difficulties, he did not become discouraged. In all his prayers he repeated, in song, "Lord, it's you whom I ask for strength." Those who were beside him in the last moments of his life, including the Rev. Athanase Musende,[2] affirm that they witnessed in 1991 the death of a pious man.

Vincent Ndandula

2 See "Athanase Musende's last pastoral visit" (chapter 88).

Part II
Christians caught in violence

25 ❧ Pierre Mulele's Jeunesse rebellion

In June of 1960, political independence came suddenly to the Belgian Congo, a land and people who had not been prepared for it. Well-intentioned but ill-equipped Congolese moved into government offices abruptly vacated by the Belgian administrators. For a while governmental affairs coasted along on the momentum left by the Belgian colonizers. Meanwhile there was celebration and joy all across that immense land. The resented Belgians were gone. Fellow Congolese now were in places of power. At long last they would be governed by their own brothers. All would be well.

Several years later, the scene and mood across Congo was radically different. While new government officials were content to live privileged lives in the urban centers, the infrastructure across the country had deteriorated. Sandy roads had become gullies under the torrential rainy-season rains. Little by little, bush stores had closed, making it difficult to secure even basic necessities of life. People were disillusioned and felt betrayed. Conflict broke out, often along tribal lines. Rebels in different parts of the country moved in to stir up chaos and take control.

Into the dry social tinder in Bandundu Province, in Mennonite mission territory, came a handful of clever agitators led by Pierre Mulele, who had been trained in China. Seated around the village hearth fires at night, they asked pointed questions: "How long is it since you had salt with your greens? How long is it since you were

---

photo—Pierre Mulele standing before his troops

able to buy a new machete? Or a lantern? Or flashlight batteries? A bicycle tire? A bottle of kerosene?" Response was prompt and bitter.

"Well," said the agitators, "we want to start a new political party, and if you support us, we're going to seize our land and throw out the worthless people in Leopoldville. When we set up a new government, we will remember and reward you all." When asked who exactly *they* were, they would reply, "We are the Jeunesse"—the youth of the land.

Easily persuaded that these were people to be trusted, village after village pledged support. Beyond that, villagers promised to provide the rebels and their activities with a shield of secrecy. Soon there were whispers in the wind about shadowy activities in isolated places in the forest. When government officials made inquiry, no one knew anything! Meanwhile scores of teams of Jeunesse were being trained in hidden places and returning to their home villages at sundown, dusty and tired and secretive.

Then came the night of January 15, 1964, when these teams were unleashed on predetermined targets in a single night, slashing, burning, destroying. In a matter of two or three days they took control of an immense area of eastern Bandundu Province. Two Mennonite mission stations, Mukedi and Kandala, lay in their path. While Kandala station was sacked and largely destroyed, Mukedi initially escaped harm because of a powerful area chief, who though allied with the movement, forbade that "his mission" be touched.

Jim Bertsche

26 ⚜ That's all you can do to me

The first warning Pastor Emmanuel Wayindama[1] and his family had was the sound of excited shouting in the distance and the sight of shadowy figures leaping about, systematically setting fire to the thatch-covered homes of Bible Institute students.

Pastor Wayindama had been brought to Kandala in the fall of 1963 to serve on the teaching staff of the Africa Inter-Mennonite Mission's Bible institute. An earlier graduate of the institute, he had displayed not only a keen mind but also a deep commitment to his Lord and to the church. When the search was on for Congolese to join the teaching staff at Kandala, Pastor Emmanuel Wayindama was an early choice.

The institute had been displaced from Kalonda, near Tshikapa on the banks of the Kasai River some 100 miles to the east, because of the tribal conflict that had erupted there after the hastily granted independence in 1960. Unfortunately, the move placed the institute in a territory where a different kind of unrest was brewing, in which missions were often a target.

On this violent night in January 1964, all along the Kwilu River, Catholic and Protestant mission posts were attacked. In the rebels' view, missions had partnered with the hated Belgians and needed to be eliminated before the country could be reconstructed for the good of all. The young rebels declared, "We need to remove all traces

photo—Emmanuel Wayindama explaining scripture to youth

1 See "A small man of giant wisdom" (chapter 24).

of what was before, so Moscow will come and help us rebuild our country."

As rebels arrived at the small thatch-covered home of Pastor Wayindama, his wife and family managed to escape into the surrounding darkness, but the pastor was intercepted.

"And who are you?" they asked him. "Are you also part of this school of foreigners that the missionaries brought here to Kandala?"

"Yes, I am a teacher at the institute."

"So you are not a student?" Pastor Wayindama was a small man. "Are you then a pastor?"

"Yes, I am."

"A pastor! That's even worse."

From that point on, the interrogation was accompanied by a hail of blows, some with fists, some with the wooden arcs of the bows and arrows carried by each rebel. Pastor Wayindama was soon bloodied and beaten to his knees.

Then the rebel team leader leaned over and shouted into his face: "You know that I can kill you right here on this spot, don't you?"

Pastor Wayindama looked into the eyes of his tormentor and through bloody, swollen lips replied: "Sure you can, but if you do, that's all you can do to me!"

The rebel leader was speechless. He had fully expected to see the pastor grovel at his feet, pleading for his life. For a long moment he stared at Pastor Wayindama, then turned and ordered his team elsewhere.

Pastor Wayindama lived to lead student families to safety across some 125 miles of dry, hot landscape, limping painfully all the way. His experience and witness are part of the precious legacy of the Mennonite Church of Congo.

Jim Bertsche

27 ❧ Praise the Lord! We've crossed our Jordan

History sometimes turns on surprising hinges. In this case it was a Mennonite layman named David Kipoko who singlehandedly turned the tide of the Jeunesse rebellion on its eastern flank.

Lean and sinewy, a man of direct gaze and deep convictions, Kipoko was a first-generation Christian from a village near Nyanga station, a mission post of Congo Inland Mission planted in 1923 among the Pende people of the West Kasai. In 1956 the American Bible Society recommended the revision of an existing Pende New Testament. The translation team was to include representatives from the three Africa Inter-Mennonite Mission stations that by then had been established among the Pende people. David Kipoko was the immediate choice to represent Nyanga. Though his formal training was limited, he knew his people, their culture, and their language—and most important of all, his commitment to his Lord was deep. Bringing his people God's word in their own language became David Kipoko's special mission.

The work was interrupted in the late 1950s by the furlough of the missionary in charge, and then it resumed at Kandala in the fall of 1959, at a time of powerful political ferment across Congo. During the violence that swept Kandala station in January 1964, missionaries were herded together and threatened with death. After three days in the hands of rebels, they were eventually allowed to leave on United

photo—David Kipoko

Nations helicopters. The missionaries had negotiated with the helicopter crews that they would immediately return for David Kipoko, his family, and the nonresident Bible Institute families.

At this point David Kipoko asserted himself. Gathering the institute's nonresident students around him, he said: "We do not know whether the helicopters will return. To wait here is dangerous. Gather what few things you have. We must start our journey back to the West Kasai immediately."

They were fifty-six people in all, twenty-two adults and thirty-four children—fourteen of them so small that they had to be carried most of the time. Each couple had pitiful little bundles of personal goods they'd been able to salvage from their burning homes on the night of the attack. Kipoko had rescued his most precious possession and tossed it into the nearby tall grass. This small case containing his portable typewriter had come to symbolize his personal mission in life. He assigned his oldest son to carry it on his head during the uncertain days that lay ahead. To add special anxiety, Kipoko's wife, Gin'a Laurent, was nine months pregnant.

They made their way down to the Kwilu River in evening light, crossed to the opposite bank, and bedded down in streamside brush for the night. At first light they were up and began their trek through rebel-controlled country toward the distant Loange River, which marked the border of their homeland, the West Kasai.

They walked single file, Kipoko in the lead. They were constantly challenged by roving bands of rebels. "Who are you? Where are you going? Are you with us or against us?" In every encounter Kipoko silently prayed, squared his shoulders, faced his hostile questioners, and negotiated his way past them. Around midday the travelers came to a fork in the path. The shorter route to the left would lead through a more populated area and a chance of finding food, water, and shelter at night. But Kipoko warned that they would also encounter more rebels. They would take the right fork, which, though longer, would (they hoped) mean less rebel traffic.

By late afternoon they approached a small village. Finding shade along the edge, the group dropped to the ground while Kipoko sought out the chief to ask for drinking water, food, and shelter for the night. Fearful of possible retaliation from rebels, the chief refused all their requests. The group slept in the open at the edge of the village and left silently at dawn for another long day's trek under the tropical sun.

As the sun dipped toward the west on the second day, they came to a village situated on a bluff overlooking the distant Loange River. Once again they slumped to the ground and were almost immediately surrounded by a group of surly youth from that village, who challenged them: "We don't know who you are, but if we find out there are any Baluba or Lulua among you (ethnic groups from across the river), they will not leave this village alive." In fact, the group included students from both tribes.

In response to this menace, Kipoko asked to speak to the village chief. After again encountering fears and refusals, Kipoko eventually discovered that he and the chief belonged to the same extended clan and traced their lineage to a common ancestor. He picked up a handful of sand and tossed it into the air, signifying a claim of common kinship and land, and he pled with the chief not only to spare the lives of the strangers among them but also to provide desperately needed food and water.

The chief replied that he would convene his village elders that night and bring word of their decision within a few hours. While his exhausted fellow travelers slept, Kipoko sat among them, prayed, and waited. Finally the chief appeared out of the night shadows. He said: "It has been decided. You can sleep in peace. I've persuaded my elders to allow your whole group to leave in the morning. I do not want the blood of the friends of my kinsman on my hands."

The next morning, after food and water had been provided, the group resumed travel and came to river's edge by midafternoon, where they bargained over fees for being ferried across the river in dugout canoes. Though they had been given safe passage to the river, they were not exempt from extortion at the hands of the canoe men. Each couple had to untie their little bundles and barter bits of their last earthly goods for passage.

When the last canoe load had traversed the river marking the frontier of rebel control, Kipoko promptly summoned everyone and announced a service of thanksgiving. After singing a couple of hymns from memory, he said: "People call this river the Loange, but for us it has become our Jordan. The Lord has brought us out of a land of death and across this river. We must praise him. We still have a long path before us, and we do not know what awaits us. We have no rocks here on the river bank with which to build an altar as did the Israelites, but our prayers of thanksgiving are the offering we lift before his face." After prayer, they shared what little food they had left and resumed their journey.

During the late afternoon of this third day, it began to rain. Toward evening they arrived, wet and weary, at a village whose chief refused them shelter and food. Rebel country was so near that he feared retribution. It was after dark when they reached the next village, where once again they were met with hostility and fear. But at last they were permitted to throw down their mats at the edge of village for the night.

Next morning, unmindful of wet clothing and empty stomachs, they pressed on. This time their goal was a distant village where they knew a Mennonite teacher-evangelist and a cluster of Christians were living. If they could make it that far, they knew their escape was assured. With only brief stops in the sparse shade of scrubby trees, they plodded along. Finally, after dark, they approached the flickering glow of village hearth fires and the sound of shouted welcomes of Christian friends.

As children were taken from aching arms and weights lifted from bodies trembling with fatigue, the weary party collapsed gratefully on stools and mats. Early next morning a bicycle messenger was sent to Nyanga. By late afternoon the following day, a mission truck had arrived and transported them all to the mission post. Gin'a Laurent, Kipoko's pregnant wife, quietly told her husband that she was going directly to the maternity, where a few hours later she gave birth to a son. Kipoko named the infant Gikenene ("sorrow, distress"), to commemorate the traumatic experiences surrounding his birth.

The Nyanga church council called a meeting the next morning to hear Kipoko's news. They were not only curious but also greatly concerned, because chiefs in that area were by that time leaning toward supporting the rebellion across the river. Kipoko's response was quick: "Invite all the chiefs and elders from the villages around us for a meeting. I'm eager to talk with them."

Word went out, and on a given day the Nyanga chapel was packed with village chiefs and notables. Kipoko took the platform and addressed them passionately. "You've come to hear news about the Jeunesse rebellion across the Loange River in Bandundu Province. If you want this mission station to be burned down and you want to lose your schools and your hospital, fine—invite them. If you want all your missionaries chased away, fine—invite them. If want to lose your bush stores, fine—invite them. If you want your young men to be forced into destructive travel teams, and especially if you village chiefs want to be treated like slaves, fine—invite them." After elaborating on his group's harrowing experiences, Kipoko took his seat.

An animated buzz erupted among the chapel benches, accompanied by the sound of clicking tongues, a sign of agitation. Consensus came quickly. "If this is what the rebel movement is all about, we will have nothing to do with it. From this day our word to our people will be to resist it at every turn. Rather than cooperate, we will relay any and all information we have to the government at Tshikapa."

Given David Kipoko's impassioned reporting of his experiences that day, the rebellion never did gain a foothold to the east of the Loange River in the West Kasai. Kipoko served with the revision committee for another decade and lived to see the publication of a revised edition of the Pende New Testament.

Jim Bertsche

28 ❧ We baptize you in the name of Pierre Mulele

At the arrival of the white missionaries, Elie Falanga was one of those curious young people who always wanted to know what was going on in his village. He was born in 1907 in Mukedi. He began to learn to read around 1927 and followed the path to baptism in 1934. After primary school, he spent two years at the teacher training school, became a teacher, and later, in the mid-1950s, was trained as a pastor. He married Marthe Mishindo, and they had ten children.

One of the first Mennonite pastors ordained in Bandundu Province, Rev. Falanga lived a stable and exemplary life. He had a reputation as a good educator not only on the spiritual and moral plane but also pedagogically, so clear and precise were his directives.

A humble man, Pastor Elie Falanga never resisted when the church needed him in this or that situation. Because of his dynamism and dedication to the good in every situation where he worked, God raised him to the position of recording secretary of the denomination and denominational evangelist. Under his leadership, the Mukedi district prospered and was greatly extended. He was a great administrative advisor. In all the big meetings, people listened to him attentively. He preached forgiveness, justice, and tolerance.

But that is not the whole story about Rev. Falanga. Around 1962, most of the Kwilu district was hit by the rebellion led by Pierre Mulele. These rebels, whose ambition was to overthrow the government,

photo—Elie Falanga

had to operate far from the government's armed forces. Lacking logistical support, they set up camp near rural villages and intermingled with the villagers. They carried a mortal hatred for teachers, priests, and pastors, whom they considered accomplices of the central government. Their mission was to destroy shops, schools, hospitals, and even churches.

One morning they showed up at the Mukedi station. They ordered the church to be closed down, worship services to cease, and all church dignitaries to be evicted. At first, no one dared resist them—except Pastor Falanga, who considered this act an outrage against the Divine. Braving all their threats, at the risk of his life, Pastor Falanga energetically refused to obey. His attitude encouraged even those who had lost hope of surviving.

The offended rebels arrested him, along with his fellow Mukedi pastor, David Kidinda. They humiliated the two by dunking them in the river, saying, "You baptized people in the name of your God, and we baptize you in the name of Pierre Mulele."

This treatment did not affect the faith of the two pastors one bit. As the Bible says in Hebrews 6:10, "God is not unjust; he will not forget your work and the love you have shown him as you have helped his people and continue to help them."

At the end of the rebellion, Pastor Falanga, along with others, reorganized the life of the church and brought hope back to the believers. This man of God took part in awakening the conscience of the military men who were charged with pacifying the zones under rebel control.

Pastor Elie Falanga encouraged everyone to persevere in the way of salvation. He opened the way for a number of younger people to find a calling, and he trained them and served as a role model. He died in 1999 at Mukedi. Remembering his courage and accomplishments, the Christians buried him in front of the church.

Jackson Beleji

29 ❧ A Mennonite rebel

Jean Pierre Kumbi-Kumbi was born in 1939 at the Mukedi mission. The son of Mennonites, he was baptized in 1955 at Mukedi. He married and was the father of a daughter. And then came national independence and the troubles that followed.

The main leader of what is known as the Jeunesse rebellion that struck Bandundu Province was Pierre Mulele, who had left in 1962 to pursue political and military studies in China and returned in 1963 to begin recruiting in the capital and Bandundu Province. At the end of November, Mulele's camp numbered more than 2,500 partisans, including Damien Kandaka, whom Mulele made a commander. Jean Pierre Kumbi-Kumbi was Kandaka's aide.

The two had come from the east, along with Antoine Fimbo. Soon Fimbo was authorized by Mulele to go back east to spread the action of the insurrection. But Commander Kandaka and Jean Pierre Kumbi-Kumbi, the young Mennonite, stayed at headquarters. Before long, however, conflict arose between Mulele and Kandaka, and Commander Kandaka prepared to foment his own revolution.

In early December 1964, in his headquarters Mulele got wind of this and sent an expedition of 120 partisans to arrest Kandaka. By night they were attacked by Kandaka's combatants and lost twenty men.

---

photo—Jean Pierre Kumbi-Kumbi (indicated by the arrow) among Jeunesse soldiers

From then on Jean Pierre Kumbi-Kumbi broke his ties with the Mulele dictatorship. But he continued on with the rebel leader Kandaka, who turned toward the east, where in the Mennonite missionary station of Mukedi all the schools were closed and the teachers were threatened, falling prey to the rebellion. The Christians in the rebel forces, including Kumbi-Kumbi, who came from that mission, along with the population of the neighboring villages, did not want the rebels to threaten the missionaries who had come to evangelize them. Indeed, the missionaries were allowed to return to North America in safety. In contrast, the Fathers of Mary Immaculate installed at the Catholic mission of Kilembe, twenty kilometers from the Mukedi Mennonite station, were threatened and killed. However, in pursuing Kandaka, Mulele's partisans burned the first Mennonite church in the country, the hospital, and all the villages.

Damien Kandaka, who was originally from Kondo, set himself up in the sector of his origins. Back in home territory, Jean Pierre Kumbi-Kumbi, the young Mennonite and aide to Kandaka, was able to demonstrate a spirit of love, nonviolence, and finally of reconciliation. He played the role of bridge between Kandaka and Mulele. The testimonies collected among those who shared life with him during the rebellion attest that this gentleman conducted himself more as a pastor than as a soldier. Under the influence of his aide, Commander Kandaka wrote a letter to Mulele to ask for a pardon.

In spite of much advice, however, Jean Pierre Kumbi-Kumbi did not agree to separate himself from Kandaka. In 1965, Kandaka and the young Jean Pierre fell into a confrontation with Mulele's forces and were assassinated by one of Mulele's commanders.

What is remarkable is that this man tried to stay true to his faith even in a context of permanent violence.[1]

Jackson Beleji

1 Jim Bertsche notes that it was only in reading this story for the first time in 2012 that he understood how close the Kandala missionaries came to being killed and why they were spared.—Ed.

30 ❧ An open Bible at rebel headquarters

By the time Pierre Mulele and his Jeunesse rebels swept through Bandundu Province, church authority was being passed from missionary to Congolese hands, leaving a new young team of Congolese officers in charge. Samuel Kakesa, the first Congolese legal representative of Mennonite Church of Congo, lived in Mukedi, where he had been born in 1936. His parents, Rebecca Gavunji and Jacob Gasala,[1] were part of the Christian community.

As the legal link between his church and the Congo government, Kakesa carried great responsibility. Among other things, because the government was still subsidizing school programs and teachers' salaries, large sums of money moved regularly through his hands for disbursement in Bandundu Province. To keep in daily touch with the other seven mission posts of Africa Inter-Mennonite Mission, Kakesa had a shortwave radio in his home.

One day, soon after the violent rebel attacks of January 1964, in which the rebels took control of the territory, a delegation of rebels knocked on his door. "We understand that you have a shortwave radio in your home."

"That is correct," Kakesa replied.

---

photo—Samuel Kakesa with his wife, Françoise Kafutshi, and their child

1 See "Rebecca, Jacob, and a son named Samuel" (chapter 8).

"Well, our commander, Pierre Mulele, needs one at our bush headquarters at Malemba, and he is sure you would be happy to donate it to the cause of the Jeunesse."

Though handing over the radio would leave him without contact with the outside world, Kakesa was powerless to block them. He stood by as they entered his home, gathered up the transmitter and battery, and climbed a couple of palm trees to retrieve the antenna.

A few weeks later the rebels were back, saying Commander Mulele wanted to meet him. With no choice but to obey, Samuel bade his wife Françoise[2] and children farewell and began the several-day trek to their bush headquarters.

Arriving late one afternoon, he was offered food and shown a place to sleep. Next morning he was summoned to meet Mulele. The commander offered him a chair and scrutinized him. "So you are Samuel Kakesa?"

" I am."

"You are the legal representative of a large church?"

"I am."

"Large sums of money pass through your hands for village teachers of your region?"

"That's correct."

Tapping a packet of letters on his desk, Mulele said that he'd been receiving complaints from various teachers accusing Samuel of failing to deliver their salaries on time. The commander was investigating the matter.

Kakesa tried to explain that since the rebels had overrun their area, all contact with the church headquarters at Tshikapa in the next province had been cut off. While he was sure that the salaries were being held for the teachers, there was no way to transfer the funds to him in rebel-held Bandundu Province.

Noncommittal, Mulele informed him that for the time being he was a prisoner in their camp and that Mulele would talk to him again about the matter.

The rebel camp was built around a large quadrangle of cleared bush land. Along one side was the commander's office and workspace. Two sides were shelters for resident rebels. Along another side was the rebel "jail," small cubicles fashioned out of sticks and thatch with dirt floors and a single rudimentary bench serving as both bed

2 See "Trust in the Lord and tell the truth" (chapter 65).

and place to sit. Through the cracks Kakesa watched the bustling activities at the rebel headquarters. Teams were constantly arriving with looted goods and with people they'd brought for questioning or worse. Kakesa soon discovered that the rebels imposed harsh punishment on all accused of opposing the Jeunesse movement. Now and again he witnessed, through the cracks, someone being put to death.

A week or so after his arrival, a surprise visitor appeared in the camp, someone he knew from Mukedi. The visitor got permission to pass Samuel a change of clothing sent by his father. In the brief time they had together, the messenger passed news from home and quietly told him that in his little packet of clothing, his father had hidden Kakesa's Gipende New Testament.

Days were passing. Kakesa was becoming increasingly restless, all the while pondering the packet of letters of false accusations lying on Mulele's desk. Then one day he heard the sound of familiar voices of church colleagues in other places! Was he hallucinating? He quickly understood that across the quadrangle some of the rebels were tinkering with the shortwave radio they had confiscated from his home weeks earlier, and they had stumbled on the frequency that the Africa Inter-Mennonite Mission stations used for their regular noon communication. He was indeed hearing, in the middle of the rebel camp, familiar voices of his co-workers from other areas.

Rattling his cell door, he called a guard and asked to see Mulele right away. Granted his request, he stood before the rebel commander and said, "If I can prove to you that all of the teacher pay I've supposedly misused is in Tshikapa, will you believe me?"

"You'll prove that to me how?"

"Tomorrow at noon, go with me over to that shed where you put the shortwave radio taken from my home, and I'll prove that I'm telling the truth." Mulele agreed.

Next day toward noon, the commander sent for him. "Now remember," he said, " if you say anything that would betray us or our cause, you will die on the spot."

Breathing a word of silent prayer that today, of all days, reception would be clear and that a Tshikapa missionary would be at the radio, Kakesa settled into a chair, adjusted dials, cradled the familiar microphone in his hand as he had done so often in his own home, and began to use the call letters for Tshikapa.

Almost immediately came a loud, excited missionary voice: "Kakesa, is that you? Is that really you? I've been trying to contact you for weeks. Where have you been? Where are you now? We have urgent business with you. There is much accumulated mail for your area and we also have several months of salaries for the Bandundu teachers that we need to get to you as soon as possible. Set a day and time when we can meet you at the Loange River, so we can bring all of this to you."

Responding cautiously, Kakesa said: "I am well, but I'm not able to meet you now. I'm surrounded by soldiers. The matter of the mail and the money will have to wait."

With that, he clicked off the set and looked up at Commander Mulele. "Now do you believe me?"

Without hesitation Mulele replied: "Yes, I now believe you. You are no longer a prisoner, but I cannot allow you to leave our camp. You are too valuable a person. You have much to offer our Jeunesse cause."

Next morning Samuel was invited to the commander's office and shown a table with a typewriter and a bundle of handwritten notes. Kakesa became Mulele's typist and settled into a routine. He was good at this, so his thoughts often wandered as his fingers accomplished the assignments of the day. But one day he found himself typing out detailed instructions on how to dig a trench across a road and then camouflage it. There were also instructions on the most efficient way to set fire to a building of permanent materials and how to coerce a reluctant village chief to provide whatever was being demanded of him.

"What am I doing?" he asked himself. "I'm contributing to the destruction of my own homeland and the enslavement of my own people. I'm being used by this evil movement."

Escape was impossible. Open confrontation with Mulele in that setting would only invite death. Nonetheless he determined to find some way to signal that he had not renounced his faith or his God. That evening he went to his shelter, took his New Testament out of hiding, and made his way along a winding path leading away from the camp. He sat on a fallen log and read and prayed. This became his evening routine.

One day the inevitable happened. Some passing rebels found him and hurried off to report to Mulele. Though Kakesa knew he'd been found, he decided not to change his practice. He would place himself in God's hands in this godless place and entrust his life to God.

Only a few evenings later Kakesa was on his log, reading his New Testament and praying, when he heard approaching footsteps. He turned to find Commander Mulele himself looking down at him. For a long moment their eyes locked, then Mulele turned on his heel and returned to his camp. Neither had said a word.

Kakesa knew full well that if Mulele chose to consider him a traitor to the rebel cause, he could be put to death before dark. But dusk fell and there was no summons. He made his way back to his hut.

What had stayed the hand of the commander as he looked at Kakesa with his open New Testament in hand? Was it memory of his earlier years, when Mulele had briefly studied for the Catholic priesthood? Was it a momentary acknowledgment of a power higher than him or his movement?

Asked that question later, Kakesa had a simple answer; "It was the hand of God that restrained him. I stood between life and death during those moments. God still had more work for me to do."

Kakesa eventually was able to leave the rebel camp and resume his role of leadership in his church, despite the Jeunesse rebellion. In the process he became a major force and eventually contributed to the defeat of the Bandundu rebellion.

Thus began a new chapter of Kakesa's engagement in the service of his church and his community. Samuel Kakesa threw himself into organizing the administration of the entire community's operations. He regularly took trips on the tiny planes of the Mission Aviation Fellowship to make legal arrangements for the establishment of new schools. Although he was often called a pastor because of his work, which reflected his good Christian qualities, he was a layperson. He succeeded in reconciling the duties confided to him by the church and the demands of the government, especially in the area of education.

Samuel Kakesa was responsible for establishing the church administrative headquarters at Tshikapa Centre. Those who knew him remembered the concerns he had to protect the property of the church. His wife emphasized that, in various discussions of the future of the church, her husband said, "We ought not to demolish our mother house (the church) by our acts nor wait to be buried in its ruins. Patiently, stubbornly, it must be rebuilt."

At the end of his mandate, he resigned humbly the position of the church's legal representative and became an ordinary member of his parish. Each time the church had need of him, he always rose to the challenge. One of his children recalled that Kakesa often lost sleep while seeking solutions to the church's problems, even though he no longer had a formal position in his community. After having suffered from diabetes for a long time, Kakesa died in June 2000 in Kikwit. The church recognized in him the culture of peace, the sense of pardon, and especially the concern for the unity of the church.

Jim Bertsche and Vincent Ndandula

31 ⚘ Khongolo and Malula, inseparable friends

Two boys were born in Madimbi in 1929 and 1930 and were friends for their entire lives.

Norbert Khongolo and Corneille Malula started school in Madimbi, but both left after first grade to continue studying at the Mukedi Mennonite mission. Both loved to lead singing in church. They were baptized together.

After their studies, they were assigned to teach in different villages, but the two friends continue to correspond frequently. They soon decided to leave teaching and go into business together. Thus they returned to their native village of Madimbi to start their new profession. One opened three shops; the other, two. This life together deepened their friendship even further.

In 1964, Pierre Mulele planted his rebel camp at Kifuza, a village situated six kilometers from the Mukedi mission station. Mulele and his partisans attacked neighboring villages, including the houses of the mission station. On June 19, 1965, the Congolese national army attacked the Mulele camp at Kifuza. Pierre Mulele fled with his second in command and took refuge along the Loange River, in the neighborhood of Madimbi.

From that post, Mulele and his group of rebels launched an assassination campaign against local leaders. A list of all the intellectuals and other well-known people in Madimbi was drawn up, and they were marked for arrest. The names of Norbert Khongolo and

Corneille Malula were on that list. The two friends, along with many others, were arrested and condemned to death.

During their separate interrogations, each of the two friends pleaded for the other to be freed and offered to be put to death himself. This went on for a long time. Neither pleaded for his own release, only for that of his friend. Both preferred to die if it meant preserving the life of his friend.

But these responses only made Mulele angry. "I'm sick of it," he said. "If the sky falls on me, so be it." He killed both of the men.

And thus one could say of these friends, they demonstrated true, inseparable love for each other.

Jackson Beleji

32 ꕥ Caught on the wrong side

By the end of January 1964 the Jeunesse rebellion had overrun a tremendous swath of the territory to the west of the Loange River. Barefoot, bare-chested young men in their teens and twenties armed with bush knives and bows and arrows had cut a destructive and brutal swath north and south through Mennonite territory. They believed that if they removed all white-skinned people from among them and wiped the landscape clean of any vestiges of their presence (homes, schools, chapels, bookstores, hospitals) they would, in return, receive an outpouring of aid from the Russians to rebuild their newly independent country to the benefit of neglected rural people such as themselves.

The Africa Inter-Mennonite Mission mission post of Kandala lay directly in their destructive path. The locus of medical work, a large primary school, plus a Bible institute and a few missionaries, it was also the location of a growing church. Two local pastors, Pierre Khelendende[1] and Jacques Kindumba, provided leadership.

For many months before violence exploded, a few clever leaders had been quietly at work in the villages of the area, organizing and indoctrinating young village recruits who would constitute their attack teams. In the process they also solicited the support of various Christian leaders. They portrayed their movement as a legitimate and desperately needed political protest against a corrupt, in-

1 See "A well-ordered pastor" (chapter 10), and "All I have to give is a daughter" (chapter 75).

ept government in distant Kinshasa and said they needed educated people to support their cause. Once they were in power, such people would be given leadership in the new government.

Jacques Kindumba listened attentively and finally committed himself to their cause, in secret. But after an initial period of sweeping rebel success, by 1966 the tide had turned and Congolese troops were slowly but surely repulsing them, forcing them farther and farther into the recesses of the wooded stretches of the west bank of the Loange River. Pastor Jacques and his family fled with the rebels.

Via the African bush grapevine, word of the whereabouts and plight of Pastor Jacques and his family eventually reached Nyanga station on the east side of the river, an area where the rebels had never gained a foothold. When Pastor David Ngongo,[2] the lead pastor at the Nyanga church, heard this news, he immediately swung into action. He sent a message to Pastor Jacques naming a day and a spot on the rebels' side of the river where he would meet him. "I want to see you again. I want to talk with you."

On the appointed day Pastor Ngongo crossed the Loange in a dugout canoe and, at considerable personal risk, stepped into rebel-held territory, seated himself under a bush, and waited. Had Pastor Jacques received his message? Would he come? Finally, a gaunt figure slowly appeared out of the forest shadows. Pastor Jacques was dressed in the tattered remains of a khaki shirt and trousers. His ribs could easily be seen through the shredded shirt. Severe malnutrition was taking its toll. After a long embrace, they sat down and, in a low, flat voice, Pastor Jacques poured out his story, a litany of spirit-crushing tragedy.

He had believed, in the beginning, that the rebel leaders were telling the truth. The idea of a legitimate political protest against the distant, hated government made good sense, and he wanted to be part of it. But after the rebels took control, it changed swiftly. The pastor's beloved mission station had been put to flames and the missionaries had been forced to flee. At that point he already bitterly regretted that he had allied himself with them, but it was too late to extricate himself. He would have been considered a deserter and put to death, along with his family.

The rebel leadership became even more brutal as they began to experience defeat, he reported. By then a chicken was worth

2 See "David Ngongo: From houseboy to great leader" (chapter 35).

more than a human life. Moreover, there was nothing left for Pastor Jacques to return to. The Kandala mission post lay in ruins. A roofless chapel and school buildings stood empty. The once neat station was now overgrown with wild grass and weeds. Except for a few who were with him in the forest, the Kandala Christians were scattered far and wide.

When Pastor Jacques at last fell silent, Pastor Ngongo quickly responded. He reminded his friend that no matter what he'd done, God was ready to respond in forgiveness to a prayer of penitence. God's grace was more than sufficient to restore peace to his tormented spirit. Pastor Ngongo urged him to set a time for a second rendezvous and to bring his wife and surviving children with him so they could be helped to escape across the river. Christians at Nyanga station would welcome them with open arms and feed, clothe, and care for them. The family would receive help to find their way back to peace of mind and heart.

Pastor Jacques's eyes were deep pools of longing and suffering as he considered this offer. Finally he replied, "Thank you, my brother, for your love and the love of the Nyanga Christians, but I can't. I just can't."

They embraced a second time. Then Pastor Jacques turned and made his way back into the shadows of the riverside forest, while Pastor Ngongo, with an aching heart, stepped into the dugout that would take him back to the safety of the other shore before sundown.

What caused Pastor Jacques to reject the offer of escape? Was it shame? Remorse? Despair? Fear of retaliation against members of his extended clan who were still with him in the forest? We will never know. Today Pastor Jacques, his wife, and several of his children lie buried in unmarked graves somewhere in the forested stretches of the west bank of the Loange River.

Jim Bertsche

33 ❧ I'm a member of the Jesus tribe

The missionaries at Ndjoko Punda soon discovered that the quiet student named Kuamba had unusual musical gifts. One day one of the missionary ladies invited him to join her in the station chapel, where she lifted the lid on the pump organ and laid some sheets of paper before him with straight lines and funny marks meandering over them. She explained that each mark on the sheets indicated a particular key on the organ. Anyone who learned to read the marks could eventually play the organ. Was Kuamba interested? He immediately accepted.

She gave him a few lessons and then permission to go to the chapel at free times to practice. Kuamba took it from there on his own. In time he became the organist for worship services and director of a student choir.

But the trait that most impressed church leaders was his ability to sit with fearful village people, listen quietly, and gently lead them, through scripture, counseling, and prayer, to peace and faith in Jesus. Kuamba was proposed as a pastoral candidate at an annual assembly of Mennonite Church of Congo and was approved for ordination.

For some years he and his wife lived on the station where he taught part time in the local Bible school and served as one of the station pastors. Then one day he was called to the church office. The missionaries and church leaders waiting had a proposal for him.

---

photo—Charles Kuamba teaching Congolese geography

They were ready to start a new mission at Tshikapa. Archie Graber, the missionary builder[1] was staking out a particular site. But it was even more important to find African pastors who could move into that complex setting and begin planting churches. Of particular interest was a thriving commercial area on the east bank of the Kasai where two major tribes came together, the Lulua and the Baluba. Both spoke essentially the same language, and both, according to tribal legend, stemmed from the same ancestral grandmother. But the Lulua were recognized as the historical occupants of the area. The Baluba had migrated from the southeast, attracted by opportunities for schooling, vocational training, and jobs.

On the surface the two tribes appeared to acknowledge each other as cousins and to live in peace. The Lulua were inclined to be agrarian, content to live in their villages tending their fields and flocks, while the Baluba were eagerly pursuing all options for advancement by education and job training under the Belgians.

Pastor Kuamba was Lulua. But the church leaders asked him to consider planting a church in Tshikapa, on the east bank of the Kasai, where *all* tribes would be welcome, including Baluba migrants. In his quiet, careful manner, he asked for time to discuss the proposal with his wife and, above all, to pray about it.

In his response he first observed that he knew the area well since he had friends and relatives there. "We all know that the challenges there are great, but we also know that the need is even greater. We've been praying for years that the Lord would open a door for us. That door is now open. We must act. If you, my brothers, feel God has given me gifts that I can use there, we are willing to go."

From day one Pastor Kuamba made it clear that he had come to start neither a Lulua church nor a Baluba church nor any other ethnic church. His new church would be open to anyone who wanted a place to pray, a place to learn about Jesus, and a place of fellowship and support. People began to seek him out not just on Sundays but through the week as well. He always had time for them. They left feeling not only that the pastor had listened carefully but also that he cared. With the help of the mission a neat, permanent chapel was soon built to accommodate his growing mixed congregation.

All the while there was political turmoil in the Belgian Congo. While the colonial era was drawing to a close in black Africa, the Bel-

1 See "Let's see if Archie is available" (chapter 13).

gians seemed unaware of it. Overtaken by events, the date of June 30, 1960, was hurriedly set as the time when Congo would also be granted its political independence, although there had been little preparation for it. Within weeks the black police force mutinied against their white officers, blood stained some streets in Leopoldville, and most of the white population fled across the closest borders. This triggered repercussions across the entire country.

In Tshikapa one result was that long-simmering animosity between the Lulua and Baluba people exploded into bloody conflict. The Lulua considered themselves to be in their own homeland and viewed the Baluba as squatters. Village folks attacked each other up and down a 300-kilometer stretch of the Kasai River. Meanwhile, Pastor Kuamba continued to shepherd his congregation.

One day a delegation of his fellow Lulua clansmen came to him in his home. Their spokesman said: "Pastor, we've been listening very carefully these past weeks as you preach and pray on Sunday mornings. You know that our fellow Lulua, your people, are engaged in bitter conflict with the alien Baluba among us. Though our future and your future are at stake, never once have we heard you preach a sermon that showed how bad our enemies are. Never once have we heard you ask God to give us victory in the conflict that is raging among us. Today we have one question for you that we want answered. Who are you? What are you? Which tribe do you really belong to?"

Pastor Kuamba paused a moment and then answered as follows: "You ask me amid this hatred which tribe I belong to? I want you to know that your pastor belongs to neither one. Years ago as a young man I gave my life to Jesus and when I did that, I joined *his tribe*!"

Jim Bertsche

34 ❧ A year of schooling in the forest

Sosthène Mayambi often said, "In people's stories there are visible knots where the meaning of events meets. It is therefore necessary to make an accounting of the past and be conscious of the present, in order to sketch the roads of the future." His own life was in some ways a combination of past and present generations and eventually those to come.

Born in 1938 at the Nyanga mission station, he came from a Christian family who believed in good education. He got a diploma from a pedagogical institute in 1958 and joined the faculty of the Mukedi Teacher Training Institute at a young age. But his education only whetted his appetite for more.

While the former Belgian colonizers had invested enormous resources in primary and vocational training schools across the country, education at a secondary level was largely found on mission stations. University level education was reserved, in their scheme of things, for some indefinite future.

Immediately after independence, Congo Inland Mission made a concerted effort to provide post-secondary training for a few select couples. Three couples were sent to the States. Another two were sent far out of Mennonite mission territory to Banjwadi in northeastern Congo, some forty kilometers to the north of Stanleyville (now Kisangani). One of these couples was Sosthène Mayambi and his wife, Pauline. There they enrolled in a theological training school. Arriv-

photo—Sosthène Mayambi in the classroom

ing in 1961, their studies were tranquil at first, and they regularly reported great appreciation for their opportunity for pastoral training. Mayambi showed strong leadership potential and soon found frequent opportunities for ministry where he was.

But by late 1964 violent change was on the way. In this region the dominant rebel group called themselves the Simba (lions). Each wave of new information spoke of their steady march toward Stanleyville. One morning a rebel troop erupted on the Banjwadi station and ordered missionaries to pack their bags. Given Mayambi's close association with them, he too was taken, leaving the rest of the little Mennonite contingent behind.

Upon arrival in Stanleyville, he was left in the hands of the Catholic bishop of the city. At the first opportunity Mayambi explained his situation, and the bishop allowed him to slip out of his compound under cover of darkness. He quickly made his way back to the mission post, where tension was high. The theology students nonetheless continued to follow the routines of worship in the station chapel.

On Sunday morning, November 8, 1964, it was Mayambi's turn to conduct the worship service. He had just begun his message when the chapel was surrounded by rebels. A few marched into the chapel, guns in hand, and seized Mayambi. There followed a tirade of accusations. They concluded their visit by beating Mayambi and his fellow students unmercifully. Threatening them with worse if they continued their chapel meetings, they left. The students limped back to their quarters.

Roughly two weeks later Belgian commandos parachuted on Stanleyville and regained control of the city. Excited rebels organized a forced march of rural populations northward, fleeing government control. In the confusion at Banjwadi the two Mennonite couples managed to slip away into the surrounding equatorial jungle. Eventually they left the twisting footpaths, picked their way through the tangle of brush and vines, and began a refugee existence. They lived on roasted cassava roots they dug from abandoned fields and on whatever they could glean from the surrounding jungle. At times they crouched motionless in their fragile shelters as foraging bands of gorillas detected their presence and frightened them with their guttural challenges. Here they hid, waited, and prayed, but despite every precaution they were discovered and forced back to Banjwadi, which was by then a rebel command post.

Even in Banjwadi, some forty kilometers to the north of Stanleyville, there was increasing evidence of government forces on the move: planes overhead, jeeploads of soldiers probing the countryside. Once again the rebels in charge made a frantic effort to force the local population to march north. Once again the Mennonite students were caught up in a mass exodus, and once again they managed to slip into the wayside forest. This time, however, they hid near the road, because they suspected that before long government troops would be coming their way.

Indeed, a day or two later they heard the sound of a vehicle approaching. Creeping through the bushes, Mayambi identified the armed men as government troops. He hurried back to the little group, shared the news, and declared his intention to return to the roadside. When the vehicle returned, he would step out, hands held high in surrender, and ask for transportation to Stanleyville.

"What if they shoot you?" his wife protested. He responded, "If we stay here, we will all die." He returned to the roadside and flagged down the military jeep. They were taken to Stanleyville and eventually found their way back to their home areas at Nyanga and Mutena stations.

Back at home, Mayambi tried unsuccessfully to enroll in a university preparatory school. He gave up on the idea of university studies and accepted an assignment as a primary school director in Nzaji. At the time this was a prestigious position. Teachers were highly regarded. It is said that Mayambi lived up to his position as a role model, both in his comportment and in his impeccable appearance. With his white glasses and his well-styled hair, he wore as many different suits and vests as his wardrobe could hold.

God did not abandon him. A new opportunity arose to study theology in France. Back in Congo after two years, he was elevated by the Mennonite church to the post of denominational evangelist. Accompanying a national evangelist on a grand evangelization tour, Rev. Mayambi showed exceptional power in translating the word of God into local languages.

He preached the great meaning of forgiveness, justice, and reconciliation to people who often suffered from injustice. He emphasized that even in suffering, unity must be cultivated at all cost. "Suffering," he said, "should teach us to hold to the good and not have divisions among ourselves. On the contrary, it should unite us in the same spirit and feeling."

This man of exemplary generosity shared his life with everyone. One would find him at the bedside of the sick, as chaplain to the forgotten and hopeless. Young people found him a source of wisdom, patience, and good advice. They nicknamed him "Deacon," a takeoff of his family name, Diakande.

In a later interview Mayambi summed up his experience during the Simba rebellion this way: "We are here today because of the love and grace of God. I know that nothing happens to any of his children without his knowledge. Truly I once counted on four years of study in the school at Banjwadi. I went to school for four years, all right, but the fourth year of study was much different than I had expected. The Lord decided to give me a year of schooling in the forest instead of in a classroom. It was a hard year, but the Lord saw I needed it, and I give him thanks."

Sosthène Mayambi Diakande was visiting his son in Kikwit when he died suddenly in 2007. Although he was far from home, the church district of Kikwit honored him with a large funeral.

Jim Bertsche and Vincent Ndandula

Part III
A church grows from the ashes

35 ❧ David Ngongo: From houseboy to great leader

We do not know Ngongo's exact birth date, and what he knew about his age he must have learned from his adoptive parents. In those days, in many cases the age of children was set in reference to periods of circumcision, which was performed in group ceremonies at adolescence. In any case, he was probably born around the turn of the century.

Ngongo, who later became David, benefitted from the proximity of his village to the Nyanga station, where he met American missionaries and was hired as a houseboy, or domestic servant. In that era it was considered a privilege for a black person to be near the whites. Many blacks changed their status, passing from indigenous ways to modern, "evolved" ways, because they worked for white people. The young man advanced from gardener to cook.

In that time, getting even two or three years of elementary studies was not easy and allowed one to rise to the social rank of a dignitary. The young Ngongo did not stop there. He spent several years in biblical training, this time at Ndjoko Punda.

After that, David Ngongo joined the leadership and was assigned as a teacher-evangelist in charge of the Pitshi and Ngulungu villages. His work and great service to the church were recognized, and he

photo—David Ngongo

was raised to the rank of pastor. Today the transition from gardener or cook to pastor would not be easy.

When the country gained its independence in 1960, many things happened simultaneously on political and religious fronts. It was not a peaceful year either for foreigners or for the Congolese. The jubilant Congolese insisted on controlling everything, and foreigners had to leave the country. The missionaries were not spared. They departed suddenly, leaving all their property behind. Feeling unprepared,[1] the Congolese assumed leadership of the church. All of this happened in the context of the trouble that erupted in Kasai between the Baluba and the Lulua. How were the new leaders to deal with the tribal pressures, which affected the political life of the country as well as the life of the church? How could they preserve the unity of the church in this moment when emotions and tribal passions seemed to overtake spirituality?

God raised up from this chaos men capable of carrying on the work that the white Mennonites had begun. Pastor David Ngongo was one of those through whom God showed the power of his hand. He emerged as a peaceful shepherd. In the face of the killings that resulted from the tribal wars between the Baluba and their Lulua brothers, he preached church unity every day. Supported by the Holy Scriptures, he preserved the essential foundation of Mennonite doctrine: nonviolence and hope in Jesus Christ, Savior of the world. Many Christians responded to his call.

---

1 In the early years there were two parallel structures—the mission and missionaries alongside the church and its leaders. Both groups had officers and annual meetings. In the late 1950s serious dialogue began between mission and church leaders envisioning "integration," which would do away with parallel structures and create a single entity. These discussions accelerated as change swept across colonial Africa.

Following extensive conversations at the eight mission stations, a mission board delegation met with Congolese leaders from all the stations in Ndjoko Punda in February 1960. At this historic meeting all agreed that mission stations would eventually be turned over entirely to Congolese staff. But the Congolese leaders asked that certain major responsibilities remain with the missionaries for the present, while Congolese apprenticed in all areas of work. National independence and the accompanying turmoil followed just four months later.

For more on the Ndjoko Punda meeting see Jim Bertsche, *CIM/AIMM: A Story of Vision, Commitment and Grace* (Africa Inter-Mennonite Mission, 1998), 43–44.—Ed.

At the end of this period of tribulation the missionaries would return and find a church still alive, thanks to the efforts of this man and others with little formal training but whom the Lord enlightened for the edification of his work. This work would be amplified in other areas such as teaching, medical training, and the development of the deaconate.

Pastor David's courage and sense of responsibility earned him the leadership of the denomination over more than a decade, 1960–71. During his term at the head of the community, he overcame conflicts between generations and integrated the young class of elites into the administration of the community.

But this man of God had experienced difficult times in his family life. His first wife, Rebecca, bore twelve children and passed away after the last, difficult birth. His second wife, Marie-Jeanne, died childless, also before her husband. Like Job, Pastor David Ngongo witnessed the deaths of several of his adult children before him. But all this loss did not affect in any way his attachment to his God and his church. He died at an advanced age in Tshikapa Dibumba in 2005, happy to have served God.[2]

Vincent Ndandula

2 See "Do what you know you should do" (chapter 49) and "No place to hang on up there" (chapter 50).

36 ❧ A good and faithful steward

Born in 1910 and baptized in 1935, the young Samuel Mulebo stood out among others at the Mukedi mission for his intelligence. Henry Moser employed him not only as a domestic but also to translate hymns from Tshiluba to Gipende, the language of the region.

After his studies Mulebo was hired as a bookkeeper at one of the posts of a large Belgian palm oil refinery, CKE. It was thanks to the various kinds of work he had learned under Moser that he could take advantage of this opportunity.

He married Henriette Sona and they had ten children. Samuel and Henriette led a good life of peace and mutual understanding. Their family members and household guests always enjoyed good, fair treatment. Mulebo was able to set up many of his brothers-in-law and cousins in good positions.

Mulebo was a competent and honest employee, and after rendering good service, he was transferred to Matshi and promoted to assistant director. He served there from 1949 to 1963. When he arrived at Lake Matshi, as happened in many other places, this layman conceived the idea of building a church. For this noble project Samuel was aided, in 1956, by two of his bosses who were at the head of CKE. As an assistant director of CKE, Mulebo related to people without considering their origin or language.

---

photo—Samuel Mulebo

After the church was built and while Samuel Mulebo was still at CKE, the denomination placed Nathanael Pumbu at the head of it. A well-organized choir was established, which set about evangelizing.

In 1960, the Belgians in charge of the company were obliged to leave the region because of the turmoil that came with independence. They entrusted the management of the entire company to Samuel Mulebo. As a Christian and as the person in charge, he regularly paid the workers and managed the personnel and resources effectively.

When the Europeans returned a year later, they were agreeably astonished to find money in the company's coffers—the last thing they expected. They were sure they would find the company bankrupt.

In regard to all that, Mr. Mbwalungu of the Catholic church in Bulungu testified, "The Protestant missionaries educated Samuel Mulebo very well by teaching him good ethics." He added, "Samuel Mulebo was an exceptional Christian, a good man, very gracious, full of honesty and credibility."

Samuel Mulebo died in 1983 at Kikwit general hospital.

Jackson Beleji

37 ❧ No receipt? No money!

In his youth there was little to distinguish Bukungu Mishumbi from the thousands of other village boys who across the years attended simple thatch-and-stick schools in their villages and pursued further education on the CIM/AIMM mission posts of their areas. As a matter of fact, in his younger years he was easily overlooked among others of his age group. A bit short and quiet, he was content to let activities and conversational topics be determined by his more noisy, extroverted companions. But when school was in session and their teacher was up front standing by a blackboard nailed to the forest pole structure of the front wall, Bukungu was all attention. This quiet schoolboy was a quick learner. What was more, he was particularly attentive when his teacher talked to the class about "Yesu Kilisto."

Upon baptism at the Banga station among his Lele people, he took the new name of François. He was among a handful of Banga students sent to enroll in a two-year teacher-training school at Ndjoko Punda, and he then taught for six years back in Banga. He always came to class well prepared and brooked no foolishness on the part of his students. When he started earning a salary, it became evident that he used his earnings wisely, to the obvious benefit of his family. He was soon elected treasurer of the Banga church district.

It was at a general assembly of the church in 1964 that elections were held for officers who would replace missionaries in roles of leadership and responsibility. The position of treasurer was enor-

---

photo—François Bukungu

mously sensitive, requiring someone who not only knew bookkeeping but also could be trusted to handle large sums of money in the name of the church.

During a break in the sessions, a small delegation sought out mission treasurer Art Janz for his advice. His response was immediate. "I would suggest François Bukungu from Banga. Among all of the district treasurers I've worked with, his reports have always been on time and have always been clear and accurate." This was how Bukungu, the quiet teacher from Banga, was elected to serve as the first general treasurer of the Mennonite Church of Congo.

Bukungu moved to Tshikapa and began months of intensive training at Art's shoulder, working his way through the weekly, monthly, and annual rhythms of the general treasury. In the process Bukungu was occasionally reminded that "all this money is not our money, it is the church's money. We are only caretakers." His personal convictions were only deepened in the process. But after François Bukungu was on his own at church headquarters, both missionary and African communities wondered how he would deal with the pressures that all knew would be coming.

For instance there were times when someone in financial difficulty came to his office to arrange a loan. Since Bukungu had access to "all that money," he surely could help? The answer was always sympathetic but firm: "All that money in the church box belongs to the church. Sorry."

Or someone from his distant village would express delight that now one of their own had access to "all that money" and would surely respond to the loyalties of a blood brother with a small donation on the side. Again Bukungu's response was understanding but equally firm: "There is no money amid 'all that money' that can be doled out as gifts. If I did that, both you and I would be stealing."

Now and again someone wanted to be reimbursed for something he had purchased for the church. The conversation invariably played out the same. "If you spent money for the church, where is the receipt?" Bukungu asked.

"Oh, there is no receipt. You'll just need to take my word for it."

Bukungu's response was always the same: "No receipt? No money!"

Word spread within the church that Bukungu was "a man of the box" who could be trusted. The fictitious claims for handouts ceased.

He was reelected for a second term and then for a third, although officers were technically limited to two terms. This signaled the delegates' trust and respect for a man who had demonstrated unquestioned integrity in handling their funds.

Throughout his tenure, Bukungu insisted on an annual audit. Sometimes friends would question this and wonder why he was inviting trouble. His answer was unequivocal: "I invite trouble if I do not have annual audits!" Every audit came out on the dime.

In 1978 Bukungu let it be known that he wanted to retire as church treasurer. The delegates resisted, but Bukungu was firm. It was time for someone else to take his place. With reluctance the church accepted his request, but with the stipulation that he would stay on a year or so to make sure that his successor was well trained and oriented.

Leaving Tshikapa he made his way to home territory and settled at a river port named Ilebo, where as an unpretentious layman he began a business enterprise that immediately flourished. Meanwhile, he rallied local Mennonites to build a chapel in permanent materials, a project to which he contributed generously. The local church ordained him as a deacon. Then at a general assembly he was proposed and affirmed for ordination as a pastor, a mark of high respect, although he had no formal theological training. For the balance of his life he served his church as Pastor Bukungu.

In his later years he was sought for counsel when thorny issues surfaced within the Mennonite Church of Congo. He was simply known and respected as a man of God.

Jim Bertsche

38 ❧ The unsinkable Schwartzes

Carlock Mennonite Church was one of the cluster of congregations in central Illinois that founded the inter-Mennonite missionary venture called Congo Inland Mission in the early twentieth century. Sometime later a shy farm boy named Merle Schwartz sat with his family at Carlock and listened to frequent reports by missionaries on furlough. He was moved by their appeals for more missionary volunteers. But what could he possibly contribute?

He sought out Rev. R. L. Hartzler, a pastor and member of the board of the Congo Inland Mission. "I feel that the Lord is nudging me toward missionary work," Merle said, "but what can I possibly do? I'll never be a preacher or a teacher." Rev. Hartzler's response was quick. "Merle, our mission board has been praying that the Lord would bring us doctors. You could make an enormous contribution to our new work in the Congo as Doctor Schwartz!"

Merle's farmer parents quickly gave their blessing. It was the heart of the great depression and money was not plentiful, but Merle set a course from which he never deviated. He graduated from Bluffton College and enrolled, in the fall of 1934, in the University of Illinois School of Medicine in Chicago. He took with him a bag of wheat from the farm granary and a hand-operated coffee mill. In his sparse student quarters he would often grind a cup of grain and boil his own breakfast porridge before leaving for classes.

---

photo—Dorothy and Merle Schwartz

Meanwhile, Dorothy Bowman had also sensed God's call. The daughter of fruit farmers in lower Michigan, she and her family were members of a Church of the Brethren congregation where the cause of world mission was constantly underscored. By the time she graduated from high school she felt a call to Christian mission in Africa. She decided to become a nurse and enrolled, in the fall of 1936, in the training program of Bethany Hospital in Chicago, a Church of the Brethren institution.

Merle was assigned to that hospital as an extern, and thus began their courtship. When Dorothy was assigned to the large Cook County Hospital for an eighteen-month period of bedside experience, Merle, whose classes were nearby, found it convenient to walk her home to Bethany, where they both had their living quarters. Their conversations began to focus on what would happen after they graduated. If the Lord was leading them both to Africa, why not go together? On June 30, 1940, they were married by Rev. Hartzler.

They set sail for the Congo from New York City in March 1941. By then World War II had exploded in Europe. They had secured passage aboard an Egyptian freighter curiously named the *Zam Zam.* Spotted in the course of its trans-Atlantic travel by a German raider, it was shelled, damaged, and halted dead in the water. Four days later it sank. Hearing of the sinking of the *Zam Zam* and having no other news to the contrary, their grieving families assumed that they had perished with their ship, and they held memorial services for Merle and Dorothy.

However, passengers and crew had been offloaded and transferred in mid-ocean to a German ship, the *Dresden,* which became their home for nearly a month. Finally debarked in a German-occupied French port, the Schwartzes eventually were transferred to Portugal and from there made their way back to the States—to much rejoicing and gratitude.

Now what? They had tried. All their Congo supplies were at the bottom of the Atlantic. Ocean travel was dangerous. But Merle and Dorothy set about gathering a second collection of supplies and waited for the next opportunity for travel. In the summer of 1942, word came that they could book passage on a freighter bound for the Congo seaport of Matadi. Were they ready? They were! In August they finally set foot on Congo soil.

Assigned to Mukedi station, they found a small, thatch-roofed dispensary/hospital built of fieldstone laid up in red mud mortar with external cement pointing. Word got around fast that a doctor had arrived at Mukedi station, and traffic from surrounding villages rapidly increased.

Using Merle's practical farm-boy skill with tools, and a Depression-honed make-do approach, the couple put together an innovative medical complex. No autoclave? No problem. They dug out the pressure cooker from their furnishings, parked it over an outdoor fire, and taught an aide how to use it. No shiny steel beds? They ordered a quantity of African bamboo beds from nearby Mukedi village. No electricity most of the time? Schedule surgeries during daylight hours and fire up Aladdin kerosene pressure lamps for nighttime emergencies. No traction mechanisms for broken legs? Bamboo frames rigged with clothesline worked well, with paint buckets filled with sand for weights.

With the help of Belgian government subsidies, a large hospital unit and a maternity ward were eventually built and equipped, which greatly expanded the medical services they could offer. Meanwhile, Dorothy was training Congolese midwives to help her in the maternity ward, and Merle trained a Congolese surgical assistant to help him.

Then came June of 1960 and the tumult of political independence which resulted in the total evacuation of Congo Inland Mission personnel. Merle and Dorothy happened to be at home on an extended furlough at the time. In a matter of weeks, however, urgent requests came from Congolese church leaders asking some men to return without their spouses to help reopen schools and churches. But there was more. The abrupt departure of the Belgians had left government hospitals, including the sizable complex at Gungu, just sixty kilometers from Mukedi, without staff. The new Congo government was asking the church to provide a doctor! Merle agreed to leave Dorothy behind and assume temporary responsibility for this medical outpost.

Merle lived alone in a large house left behind by Belgian officials. His days were packed with activity, but the evenings were long. He had packed Scrabble, one of the couple's favorite games. So he'd get it out and play a game with Dorothy, long distance. He'd play his hand then get up, walk around the little table, and play her hand, back and forth, keeping careful score. In his weekly letters home he would report who was ahead in their marathon Scrabble game.

In the fall of 1969 the church leadership approached Merle and Dorothy with a daunting request. The Jeunesse rebellion had finally been defeated. The Mukedi schools and church life had been reorganized. But the medical part of the station lay in shambles. Would the Schwartzes consider returning and begin again from scratch? They were willing. Merle and Dorothy devoted the balance of their missionary career back at Mukedi to rehabilitating and relaunching a medical service that had so mindlessly been destroyed by misguided young rebels.

After they returned to the States in 1977, volunteer service remained the focus of their retirement years until health and energy no longer permitted. Dorothy passed away in 1997 and Merle joined her in 2002.

Today there is a special mission alcove in the Carlock church dedicated to Merle and Dorothy, featuring photos, newspaper clippings, and articles gathered during their long years of service. Their story is an important part of the congregation's history.

Jim Bertsche

39 ⚘ Feeding the refugees of South Kasai

The missionary was working high up in the peak of the Mukedi mission chapel, seeking to repair a gaping hole that had been burned through it by the Jeunesse rebels a few years earlier. He stood on a rickety scaffolding fashioned out of smooth poles cut and carried to the station from the valley below. Suddenly losing his footing, the missionary bounced his way down through the flimsy structure and landed on the cement floor below. Getting up, he flexed his arms, then one leg and the other. Determining that there were no broken bones, he promptly clambered his way back up to the top to resume his work. When he had set himself to a task, Archie Graber[1] was not easily stopped.

Archie was back in the country for the seventh time. He had returned in late 1960 to head a desperately needed feeding and rehabilitation program among Baluba refugees in the South Kasai.[2] Fleeing the post-independence tribal conflicts, thousands of Baluba people had converged on their ancestral homeland.

Sensing the enormity of the impending disaster, Mennonite Central Committee's Orie Miller made a trip to Leopoldville, sat

---

photo—Archie Graber, with daughter Nancy and wife Irma

1 See "Let's see if Archie is available" (chapter 13).

2 The province of South Kasai, center of a brief secessionist movement after independence, no longer exists. It comprised sections of what is now Kasai Occidental (West Kasai) and Kasai Oriental (East Kasai).

with Protestant mission leaders, and brought into being the Congo Protestant Relief Agency (CPRA). If country missions would provide people, MCC would provide some desperately needed supplies. There was quick agreement, but who had the background, command of language, and organizational skills to step into that maelstrom of confusion and suffering? Once again someone wondered, "Can we get Archie Graber?"

Archie left his wife Irma and their small daughter Nancy at home in the States (they had been home on furlough) and sought a way to get back to the Congo. The Leopoldville airport was closed. Booking a flight to Luanda, the capital of Angola, he hitched a ride to Congo aboard a United Nations plane loaded with dried fish. He arrived at the Protestant Guest House smelling strongly of the cargo with which he had traveled.

In Mbuji Mayi, the capital of South Kasai, he was surrounded not only by starving people but also by conflict. Units of the Congo Armed Forces of the central government engaged in pitched battles with military units of the breakaway Katanga Province on their southern border. One day a protracted firefight took place in the city just outside his dwelling. Archie spent most of an afternoon flat on his stomach under a large table. A few days later he made his way along roads lined with bloated, fly-covered bodies.

He scrounged, wheedled, and repaired a few beat-up trucks from the local government to transport the MCC supplies being flown in. By that time UN personnel had also arrived and soon were leaning heavily on the missionary in town who knew both the refugee population and their language. By far the most frustrating aspect of his work was the need to defend his relief efforts before a local government official. Jealous of what this newly arrived Protestant relief agency was suddenly accomplishing among them, the official proceeded to lay arbitrary regulations on Graber while his fellow Baluba tribesmen were coming daily in their rags, pleading for food.

Despite the crush of day-to-day problems, Archie remained focused on the long-range goal of reinvigorating a refugee population. Making arrangements with a Mennonite source in the States, he arranged for hundreds of baby chicks to be airlifted to Mbuji Mayi for distribution among the scattered refugees. He brought in iron hoe heads and scattered them along the roadside; the refugees could fashion their own handles. As he passed through villages he threw out bundles of manioc stems and packets of seed corn for planting new crops. While distributing UN tents he also passed out bush knives, so people could begin to chop poles and thatch and build their own shelters. And Archie never lost sight of the supreme need of the refugees, a word from the Lord. On one occasion he chartered a plane in Leopoldville and loaded it to capacity with four tons of Tshiluba Bibles, which he distributed along with food and clothing.

Even as he was busy in the Mbuji Mayi area, he became aware of an immense camp of Baluba refugees in Elizabethville (now Lubumbashi), the capital of Katanga Province to their south. Living in miserable conditions and existing on UN rations, they were surrounded by a hostile population. Archie traveled there for a visit and walked unannounced into the camp, despite the alarmed protest of UN personnel. His contacts within the camp were a few Baluba Christians he had met on Sunday morning in a Methodist church. Camp inhabitants were astonished by this white man who not only spoke their language but also talked about people and places some of them had known in their youth. Winning both their confidence and cooperation, Archie was eventually able to organize an orderly evacuation via rail to their South Kasai homeland, something that UN personnel had not been able to do with armed guards.

The day came when tent camps had disappeared and people were living in houses of their own construction. No longer dependent on truckloads of MCC meat, they were eating produce out of their own fields and meat from their own chickens and goats. In an equipped woodworking shop Baluba workmen provided basic furniture for the area. Clusters of Mennonite believers had been established in countless villages across the area. Archie's work was done.

As word spread that Muambi Lutonga (the "young preacher," who was now aging) was preparing to leave them, a delegation of area chiefs came to his dwelling carrying an enormous elephant tusk etched with five bands of intricate Baluba designs. They handed it to Archie, saying it was a small token of their appreciation. "You are our savior!" they said, and insisted that if he had not come and entered into the danger and suffering of their refugee days, they all would have died.

Archie retired in Archbold, Ohio, where he was immediately recruited for another project. Erie Sauder, founder of the Sauder woodworking complex, was in the process of creating a history museum on the north end of town. He needed someone who could direct a building crew. He didn't yet have blueprints. Archie replied: "I don't need blueprints. Just show me a picture or some sketches, and I will take it from there!" Thus began a partnership that was to endure across most of a decade as the museum complex took shape.

Archie passed away in 1997. Many missionaries have served under CIM/AIMM across the years. Archie Graber is one who became a legend in his own time.

Jim Bertsche

40 ⚜ Mathieu Kazadi and the new Evangelical Mennonite Church

An older brother brought Mathieu Kazadi from the village where he was born to Ndjoko Punda in 1912, shortly after the first Mennonite missionaries arrived there. Mathieu was only a few years old. This little boy would become a founder of the Evangelical Mennonite Church of Congo.

A missionary raised the young Mathieu and put him in school, while Mathieu served as a house helper. Mathieu Kazadi went through both the elementary school and the Bible school of the mission and became one of the early teacher-evangelists.

Mathieu also managed to acquire land, where he grew coffee and processed coffee and peanuts. He undertook these commercial ventures simultaneously with his responsibilities as evangelist and pastor, as well as teaching Christian ethics and other courses at the Bible school. In this role he had the responsibility to present a daily meditation in the morning prayer service. He devoted himself with all his energy to his duties, training students who would eventually become his co-workers. And as an itinerant evangelist from 1932 to 1940, he founded a number of churches in the area surrounding Ndjoko Punda.

Mathieu Kazadi was known for the way he proclaimed the gospel everywhere and in whatever circumstance: in airplanes, hospi-

---

photo—Mathieu Kazadi

tals, restaurants, and in every gathering of God's people. His main preoccupation throughout his life remained the preaching of the good news of salvation according to Anabaptist doctrine.

Fair, generous, hospitable, a defender of the rights of others and adept at linking deeds to the word of God, Kazadi succeeded in gaining the esteem of whites and blacks alike, which assured both the stability and the numerical growth of the Mennonite church in the Ndjoko Punda area. In 1958 and 1959, before the proclamation of independence of Congo, Kazadi was the first black Mennonite pastor to be elevated to the position of president of the Mennonite Church of Congo. The American missionaries took him to the United States, where all confirmed his qualities as a true servant of God.

But Mathieu Kazadi's greatest contribution to the church would come after independence. In 1961, Kazadi and his family left Ndjoko Punda, along with other members of the Baluba tribe who were expelled by the tribes indigenous to that region. They landed in what is now Mbuji Mayi after a long and painful journey that took them far out of the way, including to Bandundu Province and Leopoldville (now Kinshasa). In Bandundu Kazadi was briefly imprisoned for promulgating a "new doctrine" in the surrounding area.

In Mbuji Mayi the desolate family was taken in by a relative who was a Presbyterian pastor. The American Presbyterian Church had missions in Mbuji Mayi and the rest of South Kasai Province. Kazadi began attending the church and was asked to preach one Sunday. His preaching enchanted the faithful of the congregation. Time after time the Mennonite pastor preached and thus won the esteem of the Presbyterians, who continued asking him to speak. Soon the Presbyterians of Mbuji Mayi became well known because of his abilities.

After being installed in their own house on Mwene Ditu Avenue, Mathieu Kazadi and his wife continued to worship with the Presbyterians but in a different congregation. Many other displaced people joined him there, including a number who had carried out ministries in Ndjoko Punda. Soon that church was too small to hold all the displaced believers who were joining the local faithful. Kazadi requested and obtained from his son-in-law Jonas Munkamba, governor of South Kasai, the land for another Presbyterian church. But, having succeeded in gathering many Anabaptist and Presbyterian faithful in that place, he decided to abandon it, judging it to be too small for his vision.

Meanwhile, dissatisfied with Presbyterian doctrine, and wishing to return to Anabaptist doctrine, Mathieu Kazadi called a meeting in his home on April 24, 1962, to discern the possibility of creating a Mennonite church in Mbuji Mayi and in South Kasai. He invited his peers and Archie Graber, who had come to Mbuji Mayi for the management and distribution of MCC aid to the South Kasai refugees.[1]

This was the beginning of the new branch of the Congolese Mennonite church that would eventually be named the Evangelical Mennonite Church (CEM). It took place almost exactly fifty years after the arrival of the first Mennonite missionaries in Congo and the founding of Congo Inland Mission.

This great man of faith, known affectionately as Kazadi Matayi, passed away in 1994.

Jean Félix Chimbalanga

1 See "Feeding the refugees of South Kasai" (chapter 39).

41 ❧ A prophet among his own people

One of those present at the founding of what would become the Evangelical Mennonite Church of Congo (CEM) was Isaac Tshibangu. Like other Baluba refugees from the tribal conflicts, he and his family arrived in Mbuji Mayi in 1961, having left everything behind in Ndjoko Punda.

Isaac Tshibangu was then in his mid-fifties, married, and the father of eight children. After a few years of Bible training he had become an assistant to the evangelist Archie Graber[1] and Pastor Joseph Ngalula. His role was to teach the word of God to new pupils. He did this until he was ordained in 1946 as an elder of the Ndjoko Punda church. As such he worked at nearly all of the Mennonite mission stations in the following years, until he was forced to flee the region in 1961.

The Mennonite refugees in Mbuji Mayi didn't stand around with their arms folded, as far as spreading the gospel of salvation was concerned. Tshibangu met with Mathieu Kazadi, Graber, and others in Kazadi's home on April 24, 1962, to form the Mennonite Evangelical Association of South Kasai, which would become the CEM.[2] He was named treasurer of the new association. Without any support from outside, this new association began establishing congregations.

photo—Isaac Tshibangu

1 See "Let's see if Archie is available" (chapter 13), and "Feeding the refugees of South Kasai" (chapter 39).

2 See "Mathieu Kazadi and the new Evangelical Mennonite Church" (chapter 40).

Tshibangu made a major contribution in opening schools under the association, when it was accorded civil status in 1966.

Isaac Tshibangu had brought a number of his clan brothers into the church at Ndjoko Punda, who were subsequently ordained as pastors. Likewise, he had evangelized many other families who were influential members of Congo Inland Mission churches. In particular, he had taken charge of a number of young single men. As they found wives, the new families significantly augmented the numbers of the faithful at Ndjoko Punda. Like Tshibangu and his family, these families had been forced out of the region by the conflicts. They now became the core of the new church in South Kasai. Isaac himself was ordained as a pastor by Mathieu Kazadi in 1968.

Unlike many pastors whose children escape their control and religious aspirations, Pastor Isaac succeeded in bringing all his children into the Mennonite fold, at least so long as they were living under his roof. One of his sons, Elder Hubert Tshibangu, former national administrative secretary (1995–2005) and current treasurer of the CEM, testifies that Pastor Isaac Tshibangu was a man of unshakable faith. Hubert sees the hand of the Eternal in the fact that his father engendered so many spiritual, as well as biological, children. He says his father showed them all the way of faith, and they have never left this path. He testifies that they remain in service to the Lord in this church where they were born, married, brought their children, and continue today.

Isaac Tshibangu passed away in 1992 but left his children, his clan brothers, and many other people to carry on the work of God.

Jean Félix Chimbalanga

42 ❧ An heir to the missionaries

Felix Shakatanga was one of the pioneers whose names were linked with the birth of early Mennonite missions in Bandundu Province. However, he began his Christian life through contact with Canadian Baptist missionaries who came to Congo and set up a mission at Shakenge, not far from his native village.

Evangelism was accompanied by classes to educate teacher-evangelists to spread the gospel. Shakatanga began his studies with other young people of his generation. He soon attracted the attention and affection of the missionaries, who found him a studious and courageous pupil because in his spare time he worked in their homes. In return, the missionaries supported all his school expenses.

Around 1938, after primary school, he received several years of biblical training. Upon returning, Felix Shakatanga became a valuable liaison between the mission and the indigenous population. A competent religious teacher, he took an active part in evangelizing the territory in company with other Congolese colleagues.

In 1958–59 the winds of independence were blowing in Africa, and the Congo, in its turn, stepped into the dance. Expatriates felt threatened and prepared to return home. In this climate of insecurity and trouble, the missionaries handed over to Shakatanga all the legal documents having reference to the Shakenge station. Among these was a letter giving him power of attorney and permission to

---

photo— Rev. Felix Shakatanga

negotiate handing over the Baptist mission of Shakenge to the Mennonite mission, AIMM.

The years following independence did not make that task easy. In 1964 the Mulelist/Jeunesse rebellion broke out in Bandundu Province and destroyed Shakenge station. This rebellion also scattered those whom the departing missionaries had put in charge. At the end of the rebellion, Rev. Shakatanga and others, including Simon Mukanza,[1] contacted Mennonite missionary Ben Eidse, who was living in Kamayala and evangelizing a great part of the surrounding territory.

The proposal of a merger was accepted by Eidse, who sent teacher-evangelists to back up Shakatanga. Eidse was also able to arrange the transfer of some government school subsidies, which had supported the Baptist mission schools, to the new administration.

After the destruction of Shakenge, however, Ben Eidse suggested moving the mission to a different place. Shamwana was chosen. Thus began Rev. Shakatanga's great mission of evangelism for the Mennonite Church of Congo (CMCo). His contribution was great, including the founding of the church districts of Mukoso, Maziamo, and others.

In denominational leadership gatherings Shakatanga maintained that the church must not only satisfy the spiritual needs of the believers but also must pursue favorable conditions for people's total development. Many young people who were better educated found Rev. Shakatanga and his ideas old-fashioned and conservative, but that didn't bother him. He represented the original, conservative stock of nonviolent doctrine. Sometimes adopting a dictatorial approach, he knew how to train the young in theology and the Bible.

Rev. Shakatanga was a visionary and worried about the future of the denomination because of tribal divisions and inordinate ambition on the part of young leaders. On the other hand, he could be somewhat full of himself, often exhibiting a superiority complex as a direct heir of the white mission. For example, after the CMCo had installed shortwave radios at its stations, Rev. Shakatanga was in the habit of taking his time on the radio, talking to one station after another, ignoring the agreed order and call times.

Nevertheless, he remains an example of religious vitality and deep-rooted faith, despite the difficult working conditions in which

---

1 See "Uniting the Mennonite communities" (chapter 55).

he developed. His life is a lesson to young servants who get sucked in by a taste for comfort and ease.

This man who died at the threshold of the centennial affirmed that "Christianity and the Christian faith are a certainty that show that Jesus is really the Son of the living God."

His conviction was sure: Those who approach God and serve him in righteousness will live in paradise. "For the meek will inherit the land and enjoy peace and prosperity" (Ps. 37:11; NIV).

Vincent Ndandula

43 ⚜ A persistent preacher

Pastor Mutombo Ngalamulume's sermons were more concise than his name. The faithful nicknamed him Tshibila, which means rapid, because he could capture his audiences in a short time with his interesting messages. In the region where he was born, in East Kasai, the name Ngalamulume is often given to a boy born into a family where the firstborn are girls.

Teachers in mission schools had small classes, knew their pupils individually, and followed each one's evolution with interest. By the end of his primary studies at Lubondanayi around 1951, Mutombo showed a great interest in the word of God. He was assigned as a teacher-evangelist in 1952 in Tshibawu. However, he did not hide his admiration for pastors and his own inclinations in that direction.

He felt so called by the Lord that he decided to take up the pastoral path after his marriage with Kapinga Tshikenge. He enrolled in the Kalonda Bible Institute in 1959. But things were not easy for him, because with the accession of the country to independence, especially in Kasai, tribal war broke out between Baluba and Lulua as well as between Pende and Chokwe. In the turmoil the Bible institute was transferred to Kandala in Bandundu. But here too, institutions were destabilized by the post-independence conflict known as the Mulelist or Jeunesse rebellion.

Mutombo was attached to his vocation and did not despair. He showed exceptional patience and finished his biblical studies in 1967.

---

photo—Mutombo Ngalamulume

This patience paid off in 1969 when he was ordained pastor at Kalomba Kabuadi.

For many long years Pastor Mutombo and his wife placed themselves totally at the disposition of the community and were willing to go wherever the needs were felt. That was how they went to work in one community after another— Lungudi, Kalonda, Biantondi, Kasai Abattoir.

Rev. Mutombo gave great importance to work. He believed that the creator placed humans in the garden to cultivate its soil and to be caretakers. For him daily manual work was not a form of slavery but rather a responsibility entrusted by God himself, which gives meaning to human life.

This servant of God left behind concrete actions. He made a great contribution to the building of churches in Biantondi and Kasai Abattoir. He died at the age of sixty-four years.

Vincent Ndandula

44 ❧ Léon Kibende plants a church in Kikwit

The great majority of early Mennonite missions were planted in rural areas. The few established in urban centers were at the periphery. The most important factor was that the Protestant Council of Congo more or less divided the territory and designated a region in which each denomination could extend its evangelism. People lived mostly in rural areas.

Léon Kibende was one of the Mennonite Christians who pushed the envelope of Mennonite territory.

Kibende was born near Mukedi in 1915, went through the primary and Bible school there, and decided to turn to medicine. He went to Sona Bata in the Bas-Congo Province to study nursing. Returning home, he soon found employment as a nurse. At that time, having a good job that paid regularly was a matter for rejoicing. It also qualified him to commit to a Christian marriage appropriate to his social rank. He married Madeleine Ndungo, and they had eight children. He always said his marriage was proof of his Christian morality and his commitment to serve God in righteousness.

Although he was happy with this stable family and professional life, he had a vision of other possibilities. He decided to leave Mukedi and move to the city. Arriving in Kikwit, he realized that the Mennonite missionaries did not have a single representative there. Each Sunday he went to worship with the Baptists. But he saw that

photo—Léon Kibende

eventually large numbers of his fellow Mennonites would establish themselves in cities. They could not depend indefinitely on the Baptists and other Protestant groups. They would need to preserve their identity in the face of other influences. Gradually he developed a plan to give birth to a Mennonite congregation in which he could freely practice the doctrine of nonviolence in which he had been raised.

He started by opening a prayer cell on his own property, with members of his family. Soon others who had left Mukedi joined them. Faced with growing numbers, Kibende spent his own money to have benches made for the little church, giving his companions a lesson in self-reliance.

From 1960 to 1964 there were not many Mennonite Christians in Kikwit. But in the course of 1965, after the Mulele rebellion had hit many villages in the Kwilu region, there was a large rural exodus to the city. The numbers of the little Mennonite community swelled accordingly. It became necessary to acquire land to build a large church.

Once again preaching by example, Léon Kibende bought property for the church with his own money. Today that land houses ten or so schools and the administrative seat of the church for North Bandundu Province.

Thanks to that initiative, the Africa Inter-Mennonite Mission came through with funds to help build the church. This first step was the beginning of the significant inroads the Mennonite Church of Congo was able to make in that crossroads city. Léon Kibende's delightful example helped birth other congregations in that city as well as in others, including Kinshasa.

After a laudable life of work both in his profession and in the church, Léon Kibende died in 1971 following a short illness. The Bandundu Province church community holds him in reverent memory.

Vincent Ndandula

45 ❧ Papa and Mama of the Kikwit II church district

Louis Fimbo was born in 1918 and arrived at the Mukedi mission around 1926. He was baptized in 1936 in Mukedi and became a teacher. He alternated teaching and work as a salesman for several years and married Valestine Gavunji in 1944. They would have ten children.

Louis Fimbo became wealthy. He had two coffee farms and a cattle farm. In 1952 he became a merchant and bought a truck, which he made available to missionaries for their transportation. He was able to support the education of his nephews and nieces as well as his own children and pay a monthly salary to seven teacher-evangelists. One of his children became legal representative of the Mennonite Church of Congo (CMCo). Another is director of a primary school. Three are abroad. All are members of the church. It was great blessing from the Eternal that caused Papa Fimbo to make great progress and to be a good example. Unfortunately, Papa Louis Fimbo died in 1987.

His wife, Mama Valestine Gavunji, was also one of those rare individuals who have understood that one can only walk in the way of the Lord by fearing God and by serving him with all of one's heart and soul and by obeying his commandments.

She was born in 1924 at Luvuji, a large village in the territory of Gungu, to a family whose members often held traditional power. Her father, Mihala, was the older brother of the chief of the Luvuji

photo—Louis Fimbo

members of their clan. He is remembered as a tall man who lived with his wife, Luyinda, in perfect harmony, although they were not Christians.

Like many girls of her age, Valestine left her parents at the age of six or seven to join other members of her family at Mukedi, where she could enroll in primary school. She studied for a short period of time. Baptized in 1942, she married Louis Fimbo two years later.

As a mother of ten children, Mama Gavunji proved to be a good educator who supervised not only her own children but also many other young women who had married young. She had good memories of her life as a student and maintained a preference for communal activities. She loved to relate to groups and organizations that brought women together for activities either at church or in the neighborhood where she lived.

Because of their social position and the financial means of her husband, their house was always full of family members from the husband's or wife's side. One needs compassion to manage that sort of clan, which can be parasitical and even engage in lawsuits. Her husband, though generous in his acts, tended to be miserly, but Mama Gavunji was generous by nature. She served as a bridge between her husband and relatives who were always waiting for a handout.

After the death of her husband, even though she was a widow with limited means, Mama Valestine Gavunji was able to keep peace between the two families. She never lost her gift for bringing people together, offering shelter even to the children of those she knew only as brothers or sisters in the church.

Despite her advanced age, Mama Gavunji gave herself body and soul to singing praises to the Lord in the great choir of the CMCo, which was the pride and joy of Kikwit. She remained a member until the end. She died in 2006 in the joy of having served her God and her church, which paid her well-deserved homage.

One of their sons reports that his parents gave him lessons of love, parental responsibility, and service to the well-being of the people of God who had given him a mandate to lead.

Jackson Beleji

46 ⚜ Mama Tina

About 20 percent of the Congo Mennonite missionaries have been single women. Typically serving in support ministries in classrooms, dispensaries, and among women and children, their service has often been low profile and therefore less recognized. And yet they came with a deep certainty of God's leading in their lives and at peace with roles they believed they alone could fill. Among this corps of devoted women was Tina Quiring.

Daughter of a rural pastor and one of three sisters who found their way to Africa, Tina came to the Congo in 1950 to teach. She served first at Ndjoko Punda, where her time was divided between the girls school and a two-year Bible training program for young men who were being groomed for service in village schools as Christian teachers. The custom in the Congo was for African co-workers to give each new missionary a name. Often they would bestow an African term they felt identified and fit the new arrival. But not Miss Quiring. There was something about the name she had come with that suited her new friends just fine. She became simply Mama Tina.

In 1960 her Congo service was interrupted by the violence of political independence. As soon as it was thought safe for women to return, Tina was among the first to volunteer to go back. She was then stationed at Tshikapa, the government and commercial center located just across the Kasai River from the AIMM station Kalonda. From 1962 until her retirement in 1976, she focused her attention

---

photo—Tina Quiring assisting student Benjamin Ntumba

on distributing Christian literature through a network of bookshops, which she promoted.

Mama Tina was an energetic woman with a quick smile and a well-developed sense of humor. Those who learned to know her will remember her for a number of other characteristics as well.

Tina was always busy. Perhaps it was unpacking a new shipment of Gospels that had just come in the mail. Sometimes it was running off a batch of lesson guides on her office mimeograph. Or maybe it was inventory time at one of the bookshops. She was always somewhere doing something. The partial German expression applied well to her: "I've got no time to *dopple*!"

She was always on time. She drove a little Volkswagen "bug" around Tshikapa on her many errands to the post office, to the various bookshops of the area, and to her office at the church headquarters. Every weekday morning she started her rounds promptly at 6:30 a.m, and she rarely got beyond second gear. Other missionaries living nearby often observed that they had no need of personal alarm clocks. When they heard Mama Tina's little bug go putt-putting by their homes, they knew it was time to get up and start their day too.

Tina was enthusiastic about her work. At any missionary gathering she was eager to share news from her department. She usually had proposals for expanding the mission ministry via the printed page. She was certain that, in the long term, nothing was more important for the African church than to produce and place God's word in the hands of African believers in their own mother tongues.

Impatient with barriers to progress, Mama Tina often asked: "How can we get this ball a-rollin'?"

Jim Bertsche

47 ❧ The impact of a quiet man

Herman Buller was a man who listened much more than he spoke, but his unswerving commitment to his faith and to service in the name of Christ was clear to all who knew him. This Mennonite farm boy from Oklahoma would make a unique contribution to the Congolese Mennonite church at a sensitive time.

Herman began college in Oklahoma and Newton, Kansas, but was called up by the draft during World War II. He registered as a conscientious objector and served with Civilian Public Service units in Nebraska and Colorado. After his term of service he volunteered with Mennonite Central Committee, traveling on boats taking livestock to impoverished war refugees in Europe who were struggling to restart their shattered lives. Herman made nine Atlantic round trips with horses. He later served with MCC teams distributing clothing and food in Hamburg, Germany. There he met Ruth Lehman, also an MCC volunteer in that city.

Herman then enrolled in Goshen College and earned a degree in accounting in 1951. Upon graduating he married Ruth and they took a position on the administrative staff of the Mennonite Hospital of Bloomington, Illinois. Gifted with a clear bass voice, he sang with a quartet, the Evangelaires, who were much in demand at the time in central Illinois.

In the early 1960s he took a position as administrator of a hospital in Hinton, Oklahoma. It was here that Herman came to the atten-

photo—Herman Buller

tion of AIMM, which was looking for an administrator/accountant to oversee the mission medical program. The Bullers went to Congo in 1966, where Herman began working closely with African staff and church officers.

The decade of the 1970s was a particularly difficult period in the Congolese mission community. Amid the post-independence political furor, missions in that large country were working their own way through new understandings and new relations with their respective emerging churches.

As national churches elected their own officers, acquired their own legal charters from the government, and began to make decisions on their own, issues of finance, equipment, and property quickly emerged as an extremely sensitive agenda. It was in this context that Herman made an enormous contribution to both the mission and the church.

Having by this time won the confidence and trust of a number of African leaders, Herman, a missionary, was elected by African delegates in an annual assembly to serve as the assistant treasurer of their church. He was given an office next to the church treasurer and surrounded on all sides by African staff. His dual role of overseeing mission funds and monitoring the transfer of mission contributions to the church's own budget brought many opportunities for misunderstanding, mistrust, and miscommunication. But while the relations of some mission groups with their churches were souring because of controversy over funds, AIMM never encountered such a problem. Herman's gentle, quiet, respectful stance of servanthood, coupled with his thoroughness and command of bookkeeping, quickly won the trust of the African church administration. He continued to serve in this role until he and Ruth retired from the field in 1988.

Known for his erect 6'2" posture and his firm, long stride, Herman suffered in his later years from osteoporosis, a condition that eventually curved his back to a 90-degree angle. When he moved about slowly with the aid of a walker, his field of vision was limited to the floor at his feet. Living with increasing pain only partially curbed by medication, he insisted that in spite of everything, "the Lord is good."

Herman died peacefully in his bed in the night on June 14, 2005. This quiet man left an enduring impact on all who knew him both in Congo and in the States.

Jim Bertsche

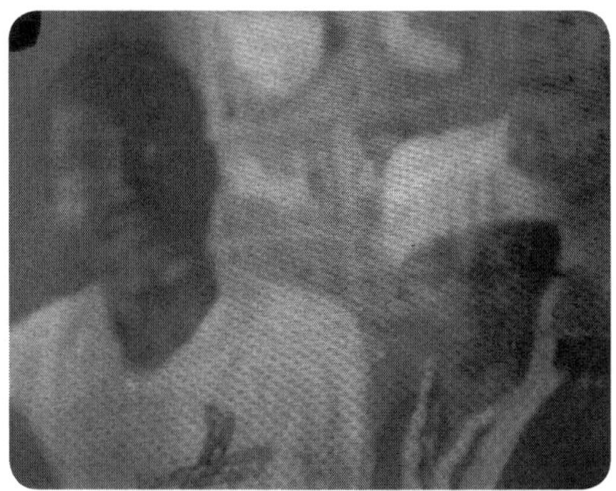

48 ❧ An excellent teaching pastor

Frédéric Kindumbu was born in 1930 not far from the Mukedi mission in a region where there were many lakes. As a youth he loved to take his little pirogue out on the lakes to fish. His parents were not Christian, but from an early age his ambition was to worship God through religious songs. All his life this tall, slender, robust man would easily slip into the kind of traditional dancing practiced by villagers.

But he is best known as an excellent teacher. He did his primary studies at Mukedi and was baptized in 1945. He continued studying and received a teaching certificate from the pedagogical institute. This was in an era when many young people still thought education was a waste of time. He then taught in Feshi Territory.

He married Valestine Mbaga in 1950, and they had five children. One of his sons became a Mennonite pastor, and his only daughter married a professor.

In 1978 the Lord and his church district called him to study at the Kalonda Bible Institute, near Tshikapa. Finishing in 1982, he interned as a pastor for four years and was ordained in 1986 at Mukedi station.

By then his contemporaries had noticed that he was a dignified, responsible man who held his own. He had taught many young people of the area and the denomination. He instructed them in morality, good conduct, discipline, obedience, and good manners, as well

photo—Frédéric Kindumbu with his wife Valestine Mbaga

as how to read and write well. He always stressed the importance of speaking well "the language of Molière." He said we must prepare the leaders of tomorrow who will be able to defend the interests of the denomination, and that we must demonstrate good comportment in our way of being, acting, and reacting.

During his life he was heaped with pedagogical honors. Besides that, thanks to his gallantry, competence, and intelligence, he knew how to manage even the most turbulent students. His qualifications as a teacher helped him work well within the denomination.

Rev. Frédéric Kindumbu sowed good seeds in the denomination. As a teaching pastor, he taught the good news of our Lord to everyone without discrimination, insisting on fear of God, devotion, love of neighbor, respect, obedience, discipline, and respect for the Ten Commandments. His contribution to the denomination was change in ways of living and modernization.

He traveled long distances on foot between Mukedi, Mujima, and other places to teach the good news. Throughout his life, he organized many biblical seminars. He was a role model—smiling, patient, a true Mennonite in the heart of the denomination.

He fell ill and, despite different interventions in various hospitals, passed away in 1997.

Jackson Beleji

49 ❧ Do what you know you should do

A series of thefts had stirred an undercurrent of uneasiness in the Nyanga church community. Some wondered if the thief was a high school student who had come from a distant place. Others wondered if it was a nearby villager, a former employee, who knew the mission community well enough to find his way around under the cover of darkness. As the thefts continued, conjecture turned to apprehension and finally to anger.

One night, the thief was caught. To the amazement of the church community, he was a son of the senior pastor of the Nyanga church, David Ngongo.[1]

A regular meeting of the council was already on the church calendar just a few days later. Because of his position in the church, Pastor David chaired all council meetings.

During the days leading up to the scheduled meeting, council members were quietly seeking each other out, wondering how the matter would be dealt with, given that the thief's father would be chairing their meeting. Would he plead for mercy for his son? Would he try to deflect disciplinary measures? Would his son become a contentious and divisive issue within the council? Perhaps, as chairman, the pastor might try to block any discussion of the matter to avoid the personal hurt and shame that a public airing of the issue would bring to him as the parent.

---

photo—David Ngongo

1 See "David Ngongo: From houseboy to great leader (chapter 35).

In African society, no loyalty is deeper than that extended to blood relatives. At the same time, the church community was accustomed to taking disciplinary measures in an open way.

The council meeting opened with devotional and prayer and continued to some routine matters that had accumulated since the last session. Finally, the only remaining item was what to do with the captured thief.

The council members were in a difficult spot. Pastor David was highly esteemed by the church community. He had faithfully served the local church for many years. Initially, he and his wife had been placed in a variety of villages to open schools and plant churches. The Lord had blessed his ministry everywhere he had gone. Furthermore, after he'd been called to serve on the station, he had spent many hours on his bike going to visit villages where he had served earlier, seeking out converts to encourage them in their faith while checking up on the teacher-evangelists resident in the villages at the time. His enthusiasm for his work, his love of the Lord, and his devotion to his church were clear to all.

When the council secretary announced the last agenda item about the captured thief, an awkward silence followed. Finally, Pastor David spoke. With an expression that reflected his sadness he said, "What are you waiting for? You know what the book of God says about thieving. You know what our church has done with other matters of this kind. Do what you know you should do!"

A motion was made and carried to excommunicate Pastor David's son and to place him under church discipline. The council also laid plans to call the son to their next meeting for reproof, admonition, and prayer, and to explain their action.

Sensing that their pastor now wanted to be left alone, someone led in a brief word of prayer and the council members filed out of the room, leaving Pastor David, slumped in his chair at the little table in front, to pour out his grief to the Lord in private and to plead for wisdom to deal with his wayward son.

The council action did not remain a secret. It became yet another witness to the surrounding community of Pastor David's uncompromising commitment to God, to his church, and to the teachings of Jesus, even above family.

Jim Bertsche

50 ❧ No place to hang on up there

It was a meeting of the administrative council of the Mennonite Church of Congo at the Nyanga mission post in the early 1970s. The council consisted primarily of African delegates, with just a few missionaries present, reflecting the new "fusion" agreement in which the mission had formally turned over administrative authority to the Congolese church.

During the previous day the Missionary Aviation Fellowship plane and pilot based at Nyanga had been in the air, bringing in delegates from isolated rural strips for the meeting. Despite carefully laid plans, however, two delegates remained to be picked up.

Chairman David Ngongo[1] noted their absence. A short flight was planned to pick them up as soon as the morning dry season fog lifted. He called the opening session to order, saying that they would get on with preliminary business items.

As was his custom, he invited the assembled delegates to join him in an opening prayer. First invoking God's presence, guidance, and wisdom for all that lay ahead of them, he then focused on the impending flight. In the beautiful, direct simplicity of African prayer, he said: "And now, *Tata Nzambi* (Father God), we ask for your protection and help for the one flight that remains. You know how it is when we get up high in the air in that little *nyunyu* (bird). There just

photo—David Ngongo (left) in discussion with Sosthène Mayambi

1 See "David Ngongo: From houseboy to great leader (chapter 35).

isn't any place to hang on to. Will you please just keep your hands under its wings. Thank you, *Tata Nzambi.* Amen."

A missionary delegate at the end of the table had a moment of secret amusement as he wondered how Pastor Ngongo might have phrased his prayer, had he had the benefit of a course in high school physics and some concept of how aerodynamics work in the flight of a plane.

Barely into the first agenda item, the council members heard the pilot at the nearby hangar going through his pre-flight warm-up routine. They heard the roar of full power being applied for takeoff. Then, after a long moment, there was sudden silence. Members of the council exchanged puzzled looks while outside an MCC volunteer jumped on his Honda motorbike and raced out to the airstrip to see what had happened.

He found the plane on the ground at the far end of the strip, less than 100 feet from the surrounding scrub brush. Just as the pilot had lifted off, he suddenly lost all power. Thanks to the timing and the extra length of the Nyanga strip, he was able to dead-stick the plane safely back to earth and brake to a halt before he arrived at the end of the strip.

The plane was quickly pushed back to the hangar, where the pilot inspected the fuel system. He was puzzled because a new motor had been installed in the plane less than a month before. He soon discovered that a little cog in the fuel pump had lost a chip, which totally blocked fuel flow.

Had that blockage occurred at any point during the flights of the previous day or the flight planned that morning, the plane would have crashed in the Congo scrub brush, its occupants dead or injured.

That afternoon the report came to the council in session. In an instant reflex, Pastor Ngongo called a halt to council proceedings and again called on the members to join him in prayer. Once again it was a short, clear prayer. "*Tata Nzambi,* we praise you, we thank you for answering our prayer we prayed this morning. Thank you, thank you for keeping your hands under the wings of that little *nyunyu.*"

This time at the end of the table a chastened missionary voiced a quiet, fervent amen.

Jim Bertsche

51 ❧ I've been invited to a banquet on Thursday

Pastor Moise Kabangy was in his second term as the president of the Mennonite Church of Zaire in the 1970s. Through his deep pastoral concern for all members of his church, regardless of their ethnic origin or dialect, he had won the confidence and respect of the sprawling church that he served.

He traveled a lot, always making sure to visit the more isolated rural areas, sitting with clusters of village believers, asking after their well-being and dealing with any friction among them. He would assure them that they were important to the broader church, no matter what their tribal origin, and lead them in a brief Bible study.

But all was not well for President Kabangy personally. He had been diagnosed with bone cancer. At one point the femur of his left leg had snapped while he was walking. He was flown to Kinshasa for emergency surgery to reposition the severed ends with a plate and screws. He was immediately put on a regime of oral drugs. Upon his release the doctor told him that his leg would heal, but the long-term prognosis was not good.

When he returned to church headquarters at Tshikapa, President Kabangy went back to work. But as time passed, those close to him noted that he was leaning more and more heavily on his cane as he walked.

---

photo—Moise Kabangy with his wife Berthine Kimbadi

Another issue troubled Pastor Kabangy even more than his bone cancer. He was estranged from a fellow Mennonite leader, Pastor Boniface Muhaku. After early demonstrating leadership skills, Muhaku was sent to the Kalonda Bible Institute and then named lead pastor at Nyanga station. His ideas about local and national church policies and program began to diverge from those of President Kabangy. After several rounds of acrimonious letters, Pastor Muhaku announced that he was going to leave the Mennonite Church of Zaire and lead a splinter Mennonite group.

With passing time, however, Pastor Muhaku's following drifted away. Furthermore, his health had deteriorated too. He had persistent fevers and was diagnosed with advanced tuberculosis. With many hours for reflection, he one day wrote a letter to President Kabangy tracing the events that had driven them apart. He expressed his regret and sorrow, accepted responsibility for what he had done, and sought forgiveness.

Pastor Kabangy immediately responded, expressing his joy and assuring Pastor Muhaku of his forgiveness. He concluded his letter by saying that their alienation had weighed on him across the years and telling Pastor Muhaku how grateful he was that they could face their respective diseases with peace of mind and heart.

The condition of the two men deteriorated with grim speed. In mid-February of 1979 Pastor Kabangy noted a small mass growing on his ribcage. A week later he was transported to the AIMM hospital across the Kasai River at Kalonda. Meanwhile, Pastor Muhaku had also been admitted to a hospital in his area. By Wednesday, February 28, both men lay at death's door.

At Kalonda Pastor Kabangy was drifting in and out of consciousness. One of the last times he rallied, he summoned his family and co-workers to his bed and said, "I have some final words for you, and I want you to listen carefully. I am not afraid of death, because I know that Jesus is my Savior. I do not hold anyone accountable for my illness and death, and I forbid that any of you do so. I accept my death as the will of God for me. When I leave you, I want all of you to remain at peace with each other and to do all you can to strengthen and carry on the work of our church."

On Wednesday, February 28, just before daybreak, Pastor Kabangy breathed his last.

A few hours later the same day, sixty miles to the north, Pastor Muhaku stirred in his bed, summoned his wife, and asked her in a hoarse whisper "What day is it?" She told him that it was Wednesday. He then struggled to tell her that he'd just had an amazing dream, which filled his heart with joy. "I've learned that I've been invited to a banquet feast with Pastor Kabangy tomorrow, Thursday. I've seen a robe that has been prepared for me. It is beautiful like nothing we've seen on this earth, a robe we'd never have enough money to buy. The robe is ready for me. I've seen it, and tomorrow, Thursday, I'm going to wear it at a banquet with Pastor Kabangy."

Later that day, Wednesday, after sundown, Pastor Muhaku also died.

Jim Bertsche

52 ❧ A one-egg Sunday dinner

The chief and elders of Tshingila village, located about halfway between the Nyanga mission post and Tshikapa, a territorial government center, had long resisted missionary efforts to place a teacher-evangelist among them. At annual meetings of the Nyanga church district assembly, Tshingila village was a frequent agenda item.

One year in the 1970s the delegates declared that though there had been repeated failure, some new effort needed to be made to establish a witness in that village. But how? Whom could they send? Among them in that session sat Pastor Sh'a Mayele and his wife Gin'a Mayele. (In the tradition of the Pende people, they were named and known as the father and mother of Mayele, their firstborn child, a son.) Sh'a Mayele and Gin'a Mayele by that time had successfully planted churches in several other villages of the area. The delegates asked the couple whether they thought they could also plant a church in Tshingila. Without hesitation Pastor Sh'a Mayele responded, "We can't, but God can!"

Several years passed quietly. Largely ignored by the village folk, they walked softly among them. Was someone sick? The pastor and his wife made their way to visit them and pray for them. If someone's thatch roof collapsed under the onslaught of a tropical storm, next morning the pastor was there, bush knife in hand, to help gather poles and thatch for a new roof. Was there a death? They brought food for the mourners. They also took the time to sit with people and tell them the story of *Yesu, Mun'a Nzambi,* Jesus, the Son of God. They always concluded their sharing with a witness to the joy and peace they had found in this Yesu as they had reached out in penitence and faith to him. Imagine! They were no longer afraid of the darkness; they no longer feared evil spirits; they no longer needed charms or fetishes to protect them.

One day there was a knock at the front door of a missionary home at Kalonda, across the river from Tshikapa. A bike was leaning against a nearby shrub. At the door stood a man holding a thumbed, folded piece of paper. He explained that he was from Tshingila village and was sent by Pastor Sh'a Mayele. As he sat down on a wicker chair, he added that he was not to return without an answer from the missionary.

Unfolding the paper, I discovered an invitation to come to his village on a certain Sunday to share in a celebration. On that day the first converts were to be baptized early in the morning. Then there was to be a worship service, followed by the first-ever celebration of communion in that village. If I could join them, I would be invited "to feed the people with the word of God."

Rejoicing at the news of the first converts in what had so long been a resistant village, I gladly accepted the invitation by a return note to the pastor.

On the appointed day I made my way via Jeep over bumpy, sandy roads. Approaching the outskirts of the village, I was greeted by several men who had been sent by the pastor as a welcoming committee. I was escorted via winding paths through the village and soon found myself approaching the pole-and-thatch chapel, which was surrounded by a throng of people. Spotting us, Pastor Sh'a Mayele and Gin'a Mayele hurried to greet us with broad smiles on their faces. I was then led to a waiting line of people. They had been down to the stream at the crack of dawn for a baptismal service. In a leisurely manner the pastor introduced them to me, person by person. In every case he shared a brief personal history, including how and when they reached out in faith to Yesu and experienced the liberating impact of God's grace in their lives.

Though the service lasted well over two hours, it passed quickly. The formal part of the Sunday festivities at last behind us, I expressed my gratitude for the privilege of sharing in the joy of that historic day and asked to be excused to begin my return trip to Tshikapa. "No, no," was the response. "We want to serve you some food first."

I tried to excuse myself without offending them, because I knew full well that Gin'a Mayele had been at the pastor's side since early morning, an important part of all of the celebration. She had no cupboard with tinned food; she had no refrigerator; she had no time to fan her hearth embers into flame and start the laborious process of preparing an African meal. But they made it clear that I could not leave without accepting food as a token of their blessing.

Stooping a bit to enter the doorway, I was ushered into their dirt-floored living room. A little table stood in the center. I was offered a village-made chair. It had to be adjusted three or four times to bring all four legs in contact with the uneven floor. Once seated I was left alone. Gin'a Mayele soon came in carrying a small enamel bowl cupped in both hands. The bowl contained one hardboiled egg over which a couple of teaspoons of peppery palm oil had been poured. She served her one-egg dinner without apology. She gave what she had and did so with dignity, grace, and love.

I've had many Sunday dinners in my life that have long since been forgotten. But the beautiful experience of that one-egg meal, served in the home of Pastor Sh'a Mayele and Gin'a Mayele, will remain secure in my memory as long as I live.

Jim Bertsche

53 ꕥ From Catholic altar boy to Mennonite leader

Robert Ngoya was born in 1938 in a "hybrid" family—that is, his father was Lunda and his mother was Sonde. His origins as well as his convictions would serve the cause of peace.

Robert was a Catholic altar boy and sacristan during primary school. It was there that he felt his first nudgings to become a pastor, when he began to identify with the story of Moses who went to liberate the Israelites in Egypt.

In fourth grade he switched to the Mennonite mission school at Kahemba and continued in Mennonite schools. He was still in his secondary school studies when he was called to go to the aid of the children of Shamwana, in Feshi Territory of Bandundu Province, who had no teachers at all, either primary or secondary. This was the beginning of his career as an educator, and it marked the first of a number of important contributions he would make in the field of Christian education.

Robert Ngoya exhibited many moral and spiritual qualities. Because the local church at Shamwana saw leadership potential in him, he was recommended for what is now Christian University of Kinshasa to pursue theological studies. From 1973 to 1977 he completed his theological formation and received a degree. This active young man worked as a pastor in his spare moments. With several friends he founded the Sanga Mamba congregation in Kinshasa, which has in turn engendered the congregations Manenga, The Dove, and Selembao.

Coming back to his Mennonite Church of Congo (CMCo) congregation of Shamwana, he functioned as prefect of studies for four years. A dedicated worker, he left behind a semi-permanent school building with three rooms as well as a house for teachers.

In 1981 the administrative council of the CMCo named him assistant director of Christian education, to serve alongside Leona Schrag. This was a significant appointment and not a random one. In his work Rev. Ngoya had shown much interest in religious education. Thus, his selection was dictated by the concerns of the March 1981 national synod of the ecumenical group Church of Christ in Congo. This group vowed to raise the moral standards of the Protestant schools, in light of the failure of the government's attempt to nationalize the schools. Two years later, in 1983, he became director of Christian education, a function he exercised until 1989.

Certain modifications in the constitution of the CMCo gave each ecclesiastical province the possibility of having a vice president. Rev. Ngoya was elected vice president of the CMCo in Bandundu Province. But in 1995 the church felt the need to bring administration closer to the people so it could be more effective. As a result, here and there new church provinces were born within the old boundaries. Kahemba became the seat of the new church province of South Bandundu. This new province was fraught with tribal rivalries among Lunda, Chokwe, Sonde, and Suku. At first this province had been called Kwango, but Rev. Ngoya refused this name, because he said it created a kind of tribal demarcation that was not at all spiritual. The name was connected to the location of a certain cluster of tribes.

Robert Ngoya, a peacemaker, succeeded in administering this entity for nine years. The majority of the other provinces sank under poor leadership and poverty because they were without reliable financial resources. But Ngoya was able to create in his province an institute for Bible teaching to meet the growing demand for pastors in the region. In addition, he introduced the church members to self-reliance through agricultural development.

During his two terms as the representative of South Bandundu, Robert Ngoya had the opportunity to take part in Mennonite World Conference assemblies in India, Guatemala, and Zimbabwe. At the end of his service, however, Pastor Ngoya, like many others, was abandoned to his sad fate. The denomination does not look after its former leaders. Thanks to good relations with the director of a school in Bandundu, he was given a post as head of the office charged with teacher education.

Besides his considerable contributions to Christian education, certain aspects of his character elicit admiration among the believers for Pastor Ngoya, who is now in his seventies. Married to Odette and a good father to their eight children, he knows how to reconcile his comportment and deeds in the light of God's word. He is sociable and likes to live in utmost simplicity. He is hostile to tribal divisions and knows how to adapt to all environments. He knows how to humble himself and how to forgive as well as ask for forgiveness. He is a conciliator who dislikes violence. In short, he is an exemplary man of God.

Vincent Ndandula

54 ⚜ Civil servant, church planter

Lay leaders have been important to the spread of the church in Congo. One of these was Fulgence Palata.

Born in 1930, the young Palata was attached to his father and imitated his trade from an early age. His father wove branches and cut straw for building houses. His father taught him the trade but also sent him to school. Fulgence was baptized at Mukedi mission in 1948. He married Bernice Kisega in 1952 and they would have twelve children.

First he worked as a teacher at Malines, several miles from Mukedi. Next he worked for several years as an administrative clerk in Gungu Territory, where Mukedi was located. After independence and the Mulele Jeunesse rebellion, he was named assistant administrator of Gungu, Masi Manimba, and finally Idiofa territories.

It was in Idiofa that Fulgence Palata noticed that the Mennonite Church of Congo had no land and had not yet been planted. So, in his capacity as a civil administrator and with the collaboration of his friend Elie Kingambo, he founded a congregation, which later became a district of the denomination.

Certain Christians gathered around him to help construct the church. Because of his energy and engagement for the good of his people, the population asked him to run for office. He was elected head of the Lozo sector, a civil position he held for many years. He was a baptizer and church planter.

---

photo—Fulgence Palata

Thanks to his services, a large number of the youth of his territory found their way to school. He spoke to them unceasingly of Jesus Christ as Lord and Savior, in whom they must put their confidence. Today the church benefits from the services of one of his sons, Pastor Jean Palata, head of Idiofa district.

Fulgence Palata died in 1997.

Jackson Beleji

55 ❧ Uniting the Mennonite communities

The late Simon Mukanza brought unusual administrative skill to the work of the church. His legacy is felt today in the lives of individuals, all three Mennonite communities, and the entire Protestant community in Congo.

Simon Mukanza was born in Kandala, site of a Mennonite mission station in Bandundu Province, in 1942. He went to primary school there and secondary school at the Nyanga station, followed by theological studies at what is now the Christian University of Kinshasa. He was baptized in 1954 and married Monique Mihala in 1962. All of their six children went to university. Three are now in the United States.

Simon taught school for a time and then went the US to further his theological studies at Associated Mennonite Biblical Seminaries. He obtained a master's degree in Christian education in 1977, the first member of the Mennonite Church of Congo (CMCo) to do so. This degree opened many horizons to him.

After that formation, Rev. Mukanza was assigned by CMCo legal representative Moise Kabangy[1] to work as the prefect of studies at the Gatundo Institute at Mukedi, which he did for two years. He was then elected deputy legal representative of the denomination in January 1980. During this time Simon Mukanza was also denominational

photo—Simon Mukanza with his wife Monique Mihala

1 See "I've been invited to a banquet on Thursday" (chapter 51).

coordinator for evangelism and church life. Under his direction, the Christian education department (literature, seminary, Bible camps) flourished. He finished his term as deputy legal representative in July 1985, when he declined to be renamed to the post.

In addition to these responsibilities, he was designated administrator of Missionary Aviation Fellowship (MAF), which provided air transport for Protestants in the country. With energy and competence he revolutionized all its activities, greatly facilitating transportation between stations such as Mukedi, Nyanga, Kalonda, Vanga, and Kajiji. He had the ability to organize and set up the entire administrative structure of MAF and consolidate its administrative relations with the Congolese state. Because of the confidence he inspired in MAF's partners and his own valuing of work well done, he stayed in that position until his death in 1997.

His energy and ability were noted and approved by all three Mennonite denominations in Congo—Mennonite, Evangelical Mennonite, and Mennonite Brethren. He therefore became a moving force behind the establishment of a new structure of collaboration called the National Inter-Mennonite Committee. Representatives of the three communities had participated in the Mennonite World Conference assembly in Filadelfia, Paraguay, in July 1987. There they made a group declaration expressing their desire to create an organization in the Congo that could serve as a channel for promoting the Mennonite Anabaptist vision of church and society and for coordinating assemblies and mutual assistance to bring Congolese Mennonites closer together.

Simon Mukanza was the first executive secretary of the new committee, which was officially brought into existence in December 1987, and he set about organizing its administrative structure with the consent of the legal representatives of the three denominations. This committee coordinates programmatic activities such as inter-Mennonite consultations, peace education, education about the Anabaptist vision, and research and documentation on African Mennonite church identity.

Despite his multiple occupations, Rev. Simon Mukanza also served as a pastor and led many souls to Jesus Christ. He helped organize a Mennonite congregation associated with the National Pedagogical Institute in Kinshasa, and he shepherded it from 1986 until his death. Rev. Mukanza and his assistant, Rev. Kwamba, did not spare any efforts to visit people and assure good training for the faithful. This work produced much fruit and led many to consolidate their faith in the Lord. They were also inspired by the evangelism of the young brother Philippe Mimbu, a beloved spiritual son of the late Rev. Mukanza who was also full of zeal and charisma for the work of the Lord. He was a youth well prepared for continuing this work.

Many other young leaders in the church felt the first stirrings of their callings in the youth Bible camps Simon Mukanza initiated in 1982 in the Nyanga district. In general, Simon Mukanza was incontestably a responsible leader, full of initiatives and the ability to bring peace within the CMCo. He was a man of great vision.

Jackson Beleji

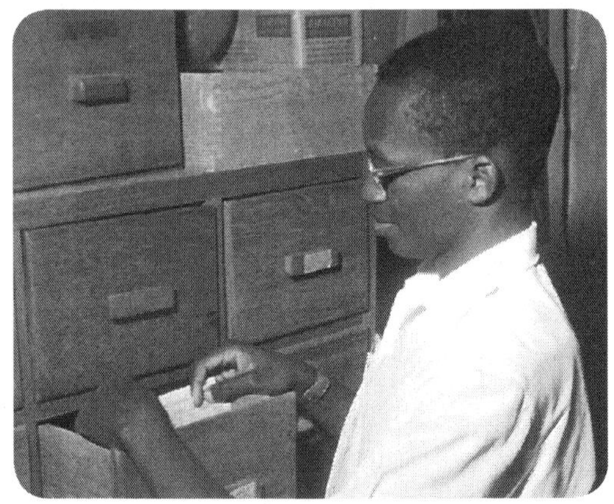

56 ❧ A new young church in Kinshasa

After independence many young people moved to Kinshasa to find work. The result was that a considerable number of former Mennonite mission students ended up living in the capital. Among these new residents were Paul Kadima, a former professor at the Nyanga pedagogical institute, and his family.

The first new residents founded an association, Former Students of Ndjoko Punda. They soon added former students from Nyanga, Mukedi, Kamayala, and Kandala missions and changed the name to Former Mennonite Students of Congo. Their precise objectives were to help one another in their social and spiritual lives, help graduates of these schools find work, and combat tribal discrimination.

As the group grew in numbers, they felt the need to add worship to their activities. They addressed the denominational leadership and received authorization to gather in the name of the Mennonite church. On the initiative of Kadima and others, the Mennonite Church of Congo was established in Kinshasa. Paul Kadima was ordained pastor because of his leadership and ability to train his peers.

The young pastor gained notice for his conduct in his family as well as in the congregation. As a boy who was respectful of his parents, he never allowed his mother to walk up hills to get water. Although this was always a woman's duty, he took it on himself. He led the choir and composed songs for it. He encouraged his friends to gather around him and other pastors and help with their work

---

photo—Paul Kadima

for the congregation. He said, "A servant of God is not equipped to respond alone to all the needs of the church. We are obliged to be at the side of the pastor for other responsibilities, so that the servant of God will have plenty of time to prepare good biblical messages."

Hearing of this, one pastor felt the need to meet this young man and his parents in order to thank them and learn where he had gotten this idea. The whole denomination rejoices in his initiative to found the CMCo in Kinshasa, which was outside of territory marked out for Mennonites. Pastor Paul Kadima is still living.

Jackson Beleji

57 ❧ A pioneer in West Kasai

Oscar Kanda was born in 1935 to Catholic parents. Moving from Catholic to Protestant, he wandered from the Presbyterians to the Evangelical Mennonite Church, having also been with the Mennonite Church of Congo. Justifying these moves, he explained that he left the Presbyterians because he didn't find love of neighbor in this group, and social life there was characterized by relaxed moral standards. As far as the Mennonite Church of Congo is concerned, he left the church because of conflicts that had made their home there and that set leaders against each other. Without wanting to be, he became implicated in these conflicts. This situation revealed to Oscar that another Mennonite church existed in Congo.

He discovered this through state officials who had been called on to judge the church conflicts. They said that this latter church, the Evangelical Mennonite Church (CEM), worked in peace and harmony. They told him that if he joined this group, he would be able to work in tranquility. They indicated that this church's headquarters was in Mbuji Mayi in East Kasai. Learning this motivated Oscar and the group that was with him to write to CEM leaders to express their desire to belong to their ecclesiastical community. They received a positive response. In this way, worship services of the CEM began anew in Kananga, where he lived, which is in West Kasai. A previous CEM group had been formed in 1985 but disbanded.

photo—Oscar Kanda Makanda

However, Pastor Kanda's new CEM congregation was at first looked down on by believers both within CEM and outside it, because they only had a small number of members and were without denominational identity or church locale. It seemed to others as if this was a gathering of children pretending to behave as adults. As their leader, Oscar Kanda had the understanding, perseverance, and determination to forge ahead in intercessory prayer. With the cooperation of others and the help of God, he succeeded in giving form and life to this group that he had brought back into existence.

Responding to his prayers, God accomplished miracles with Oscar, as in ancient times. This fact encouraged him personally and consolidated his faith in God. We can give as examples the following:

- A child was miraculously healed after a strong intercessory prayer, despite the fact that the suffering child's mother and passersby saw death coming to the child.
- Following three days of strong prayers, a local pastor's wife who was afflicted with strong and interminable hemorrhaging was healed.
- Serpents sent against certain congregational members were neutralized, as was the *tunsonda,* a kind of magic rifle used to miraculously kill anyone whom one wants to eliminate. For these cases, Oscar says, "the authors of these ignoble acts came, in most cases, to confess their wrong actions and ask forgiveness."

Because of his determination to advance the work of the Lord, Pastor Oscar Kanda also traveled in 2006 to Ilebo, a region situated 400 kilometers from Kananga. Accompanied by other believers, he exhorted and encouraged the brothers and sisters of this region to reverse their earlier decision to abandon Mennonite faith. In order to make real this noble project, Oscar and his companions brought them Bibles, songbooks, and other legal and community documents, such as minutes from General Council meetings—all of which were meant to help them understand the current state of CEM. Because of this undertaking, the Mennonites of CEM Ilebo succeeded in creating congregations including Ditalala, Lumu Luimpe, and Kapimbi, which now belong to the missionary district of North Kasai. Oscar Kanda undertook similar actions for the CEM missionary district of South Kasai.

Through sustained effort, Pastor Oscar Kanda is the one who laid the foundations for CEM's presence in West Kasai. As such, he served as provincial delegate for CEM West Kasai. But out of respect for God's word and the juridical texts guiding CEM, Pastor Kanda calmly ceded the position of provincial delegate to Robert Ngoyi. Since that time, he has played the role of director of the department of Christian education for the Kasai Center district.

Oscar Kanda recognizes that development is crucial in order for the church to avoid asking for handouts. He understands that with agriculture and animal husbandry the church in general and Kasai Center in particular would be able to care for its own needs. He underlines, however, that today's church is experiencing technical difficulties on the road to self-sufficiency—things like the nonpayment of salaries, the state of the roads, the lack of means of transportation. And other elements are slowing the takeoff. But Oscar has the conviction that, as God has done with Anabaptist Mennonites in the past, God will assist CEM Congo in general and CEM Kasai Center in particular.

Jean Félix Chimbalanga

Part IV
Anabaptist testimonies

58 ❧ A great pastor who turned the other cheek

The son of a messenger of a great chief, Onésime Mpoyi Tshiakatumba was born in Tshibata in 1918. He would go on to serve God as an evangelist, elder, and ordained pastor of the Evangelical Mennonite Church in South Kasai, his province of origin. He evangelized many people into Anabaptism and founded local churches, of which the most important, Kasekeyi, is the pride of the denomination today. He also demonstrated the way of peace through his life.

Onésime Mpoyi had an unhappy childhood. After his biological father's death, Onésime Mpoyi's mother had been inherited as a wife by his father's younger brother. The degrading and inhumane treatment that she received from her second husband left a strong imprint on Onésime Mpoyi's life.

His moves from one place to another illustrate the kind of journey, pressures, and incentives that were common to many in the region. He began primary school with the Presbyterians in his home territory but, like many others, migrated during his studies and ended up in Ndjoko Punda among the Mennonites and far from his native village. There he joined the Mennonite Church of Congo (CMCo). After completing a year in the Bible school in 1939, Onésime Mpoyi left Ndjoko Punda for Tshikapa, then in 1940 he became an evangelist at the Mennonite mission station at Mutena. Ten years later, for purely economic reasons he left Tshikapa Center for Muene Kalu.

photo—Onésime Mpoyi Tshiakatumba

There he was completely occupied by his work in the fields, and he brought in Edouard Munsensa to carry on the work at Muene Kalu. At that point Onésime only had two small children of his own, a boy and a girl.

Edouard Munsensa began his work in a church building constructed by the villagers with Mpoyi's encouragement. However, he was under Onésime Mpoyi's care, though the church provided for his needs because he was both teacher and evangelist. Since Onésime Mpoyi was a landowner, his contribution consisted of giving permission to Edouard to farm some land. The church at Muene Kalu was dependent on the Kalonda mission station.

In 1959, because of the coming war between the Baluba and Lulua tribes, Onésime Mpoyi left Muene Kalu for Tshikapa Center. There he joined the Mennonite church at Kalonda. Four years later, in 1964, because of continuing tribal tensions Onésime Mpoyi said goodbye to Tshikapa and to his friends at Kalonda and returned to his province of origin—more precisely, to his native Bakwa Muala. As soon as he arrived, Onésime Mpoyi was the target of invitations from officials of the Presbyterian church in the seat of his native territory.

He accepted their invitation and was designated evangelist and ordained church elder in 1966. At this point, having discovered that the Mennonite church existed already at Mbuji Mayi, Elder Onésime, whose gentleness, sense of service, and fervor witnessed to his call to God's service, resolved to join it. He went to see his Presbyterian leaders, from whom he sought and obtained, with difficulty, permission to leave.

Onésime Mpoyi quickly went to meet Mathieu Kazadi,[1] president of the new Mennonite group that would become the Evangelical Mennonite Church (CEM), and his staff, to whom he explained his desire to serve the Lord with them. They agreed to his request and directly named him elder of the Bitanda congregation, which needed to be organized. In 1972, following his remarkable evangelistic work, Elder Onésime was consecrated pastor by Mathieu Kazadi. His service to God as a pastor resulted in the conversions of several dozen souls and helped in the construction of the first worship building for the congregation.

---

1 See "Mathieu Kazadi and the new Evangelical Mennonite Church" (chapter 40).

Onésime Mpoyi was transferred in 1973 from Bitanda to Kabwe, about fifteen kilometers from Bitanda toward Mbuji Mayi. There Pastor Onésime again accomplished a great deal. He exhorted the faithful and evangelized local people, and several souls were won for Christ. The congregation, which was dormant before his arrival, became strong and viable.

Following bumps in the road created by leadership conflict within the CEM beginning in 1975, and given the difficulties of taking responsibility for his family—now ten children—the pastor decided after two years to leave Kabwe for Kabuela. This 115-kilometer move was not in order to serve the Lord but because of a desire to improve his situation. Rosalie Kapinga, his wife, had visited the area, and she encouraged him to make this move because the region was good for agriculture. Though he settled at Kabuela with his family, Onésime Mpoyi was obliged to commute between this location of the Kanyok people, which was becoming a city, and Kabwe, because Kabwe remained the congregation to which the church had sent him. He had not been sent to Kabuela by the church.

Finally, having made the decision to stay at Kabuela, Onésime Mpoyi was obliged by CEM authorities to find someone who could replace him at Kabwe. He decided on Elder Nsenga, one of those whom he had evangelized and consecrated. At Kabuela, Pastor Onésime succeeded in gathering a group of men and women with whom he established an evangelical circle. As pastor, he taught them Anabaptist doctrine.

Five years later, a bad wind began to blow in the new Kabuela congregation. Elder Shambuyi Buzanga, the pastor's assistant, who was of Presbyterian origin, saw and understood that almost all the members were of like origin. After manipulating them, he proposed a vote between himself and Pastor Onésime in order to determine who would lead the church. Faced with this confusion, behind which lay the unexpressed desire to replace Anabaptism with Buzanga's Presbyterianism, Onésime Mpoyi, who was naturally a calm and humble man, decided on a different path. Instead of allowing a vote with his rival, motivated by bad intentions, Onésime Mpoyi chose to relinquish the congregation he had founded to his detractor. "Instead of disputing between ourselves and going to a vote, as you desire, since the harvest is vast I will leave the congregation to you. It's up to you to calmly nourish the Lord's sheep. As for me, I will go where the Lord will lead me."

Still feeling called, with the mission to announce the good news of Christ according to Anabaptist understandings, he went to see the chief of a community about three kilometers from his residence, in order to request the use of some land. During this period of negotiations Onésime Mpoyi already began to evangelize in this area. He succeeded in winning for Christ the chief himself as well as the chief's wife, to whom Onésime Mpoyi gave the responsibility of deaconess for the new assembly. In this work, which he carried out together with his children, he evangelized a number of others who, along with Pastor Onésime's children, gathered on the veranda of the chief's house.

Several days later, the chief responded to the request for land and granted to Pastor Onésime a plot of three hundred meters by one hundred meters. Onésime Mpoyi and his children, focusing on their mission, cleared the land for construction, while still living at their home three kilometers away. His sons worked to build their own homes and the house of the Lord. In 1981, with the help of his sons and some church members, Pastor Onésime built the first church building out of palm branches. With the construction of this shelter functioning as a meeting place for Kasekeyi, this acquired space began little by little to be transformed and to attract people.

In the course of this same year, Pastor Onésime, still assisted by his children, planned and began construction of the new church building to replace the initial shelter with something more permanent. Everyone began by making adobe bricks. This initiative exclusively from his family ended with the construction of the brick church building with a straw roof. His son Fortunat, a mason's apprentice, worked on the walls, while Pastor Onésime and the younger brothers made the roof.

Concerned with the image of a church well built on its foundation, and in order to properly develop the land he had received, Pastor Onésime and his sons, who were by this time all married and responsible, decided to live on the land received, on which some immigrants had already squatted. The building on the land, the evangelical actions undertaken, and the construction of the new church building in adobe brick and straw, larger than the initial shelter, attracted a lot of attention and reflected the viability of the congregation.

From this time, the Kasekeyi congregation became visible. Onésime Mpoyi was the shepherd. Dozens of souls were won to Christ. The church was organized and well administered by its founder. He gave it a particular form by organizing the community into work groups.

CEM leaders did not visit this congregation during its first fourteen years, but Onésime Mpoyi was not discouraged and did not neglect to send regular reports of its activities. However, several years after the church was established, it was once again attacked by Shambuyi Buzanga and followers of Pastor Zacharie Nkumbi. These latter fiercely took him to court, intending by any means possible to take away the congregation in order to replace Onésime Mpoyi with someone from their group. Buzanga for his part was seeking to take over this congregation as well for the Presbyterians. Alone, with courage, Onésime resisted them all. This time, no one succeeded in taking away what he himself had sought and founded.

Rev. Onésime Mpoyi began tirelessly to evangelize the surrounding villages. In 1988 he established the Malombolombo congregation. He gave leadership of this group to Mr. Kantole wa Kantole, a Presbyterian whom he consecrated as a Mennonite pastor. Soon afterward, with the help of one of Kasekeyi's members, Pastor Onésime succeeded in evangelizing Kamayi Matoke, an agricultural hamlet seven kilometers from Kasekeyi, and established a congregation of the same name there. After its establishment, he worked there himself at first, and then later sent missionaries for short periods. Finally he gave management of this congregation to the Bondoyi missionary district, which placed Elder Mukuna Luvungula of the CEM Bufuki congregation there as shepherd.

Around 1990 Onésime Mpoyi, along with members of his first congregation, initiated and completed Kasekeyi, an agricultural project. They established fields for the congregation and also worked in others' fields, which earned them money. With the proceeds from this work the congregation purchased a goat. Profits from the goat's offspring enabled the congregation to begin constructing a church building with a tin roof. They were also able to mourn and bury the dead of the congregation with the proceeds of this project. Today the congregation boasts over 300 worshipers—men, women, and youth.

During his entire life and career, Pastor Onésime Mpoyi Tshiakatumba was highly esteemed by many, both Christians and non-Christians. Mathieu Kabanga, a member of his congregation, testifies, "Pastor Mpoyi has never done anything that did not give joy to my heart, whether in his ministry or in his social and family life. His greatest merit is that he showed all his children the way of the Lord, and they are up to today influential members of CEM."

Strongly characterized by a permanent concern to seek peace and reconciliation, Pastor Onésime was a great counselor for members of the church, people outside the church, and his biological family. François Mbuyi, one of his collaborators, underlines, "Throughout his life, Pastor Mpoyi never had a problem with anyone. He's been without reproach all along. He was very humble and respected everyone, old and young. He had a deep sense of forgiveness, even when he had been cruelly offended." To illustrate all of this, François testifies, "Mpoyi's wife died a death that may have been caused by someone well known, as people believed. But instead of taking this man to court or avenging himself, as he could have done, he forgave the wrong and asked his sons to do the same, because he considered that God alone has the power to avenge for themselves and for their mother. This is a powerful testimony, for Rosalie Mbuyi's executioner lives peaceably in Kabuela." François concludes, "Because of this act, many have believed that Pastor Tshiakatumba was truly a man of God and that he will rise again on the last day when the trumpet will sound."

Having become weak because of age, in 1999 Onésime Mpoyi wrote a letter to the CEM General Council, in which he requested that Pierre Ndibu Shambuyi replace him in his congregation. Pierre was one of those who had made up and directed the group that had chased him from Kasekeyi. Onésime Mpoyi welcomed Pierre kindly and handed over to him all the administration of the congregation, without taking into account Pierre's earlier efforts to overthrow him. Though Pierre did not do an exceptional job with the congregation, Onésime Mpoyi made every effort to create a peaceful life for him and give him ongoing moral support.

Besides what he accomplished in his cherished Kasekeyi, Onésime Mpoyi served God as the community development director for the missionary district of Bondoyi, which was led by Pastor Célestin Kabengela.[2] His initiatives, counsel, and actions brought many advantages to the district and to his congregation. Pierre Ndibu affirms, "It was in 1994, after CEM's Provincial Council meeting and the Bondoyi district meeting during which he was elected community development director, that I began to appreciate the qualities of this servant of God. What struck me strongly was the value of his sermons, the precious nature of his counsel, and the depth of his arguments during the different levels of meetings. He was very wise, and there was nothing to reproach him."

Along the same lines, Pastor Mpoyi was elected superintendant of the ecumenical group, Church of Christ in Congo, for the Kanda Kanda sector. As such, he led a large spiritual and social life. Mathieu Kabanga spoke to this subject: "In his social life, Tshiakatumba lived well with others. Many came to him to learn biblical truths. This was the case for pastors from the Malemba church, the Communion church, Unity and Fraternity, the Neo-Apostolic church, and others. It was because of his renown in pastoral ministry and his reputation that he attracted such esteem."

Constantly linking words and actions as a practicing believer, Pastor Onésime was passionate about loving his neighbor. A generous man, his habit was to share food, agricultural produce, and goods of various kinds with others: members of the church, young and old; those who lived in his town of Kabuela; and strangers who showed up at the church or at his home. "Pastor Mpoyi Tshiakatumba was a formidably generous man. He shared bed and food with mentally challenged individuals from his village. That affected us greatly, we his children, and moved us to do likewise," states his son Gustave Tshivuila.

Michel Mbuyi, secretary of the Kasekeyi congregation, reports, "A sick, mentally challenged man named Papa Kalala was brought to our congregation by villagers who were convinced of the hospitality and generosity of Pastor Mpoyi. Mpoyi welcomed him and saw that he was ill. Thereafter Pastor Mpoyi stayed at his bedside in the church building, from the time he was brought in until the day he gave up his soul. He prepared the body and buried this man, after having clothed him with his own clothing, fed him at his own expense, and provided some small health care for about two weeks." Continuing, Michel Mbuyi states, "Pastor Mpoyi astonished many

2 See "Saved from suicide by a vision" (chapter 70).

in this village, ourselves included, when he welcomed, lodged, and fed in this church building, for almost two months, more than twenty Hutu refugees from Rwanda who had wandered into East Kasai Province following the genocide that their country had experienced in 1994. Despite the fact that he himself was old and weak, Pastor Onésime fed and gave produce such as sweet potatoes from his meager means to these unfortunate people, nine families."

To seal yet more his life of attachment and service to God, Rev. Onésime Mpoyi did not cease to tell his contemporaries and those who had been converted by the message he shared: "Stay attached to Jesus Christ who is Lord and Savior, and avoid quarrels within the church. Consider yourselves as brothers and sisters."

Pastor Onésime Mpoyi Tshiakatumba passed away on December 2, 2007.

Jean Félix Chimbalanga[3]

3 Jean Félix Chimbalanga is Onésime Mpoyi's son.

59 ⚜ The desire to belong to one body

After he had been away at school, Pascal Blaise Misakayabo returned in 1972 to Mbuji Mayi, his town of origin, to serve his church, the Evangelical Mennonite Church (CEM). Mbuji Mayi is the seat of the CEM. But things were not going well. A huge leadership conflict had broken out, opposing Pastor Zacharie Nkumbi to pastors Mathieu Kazadi, André Ntumba, and a number of others. Pascal was obliged by the circumstances to define himself relative to this disaster. He found himself on the side of Kazadi and Ntumba, and the two leaders were instrumental in obtaining a scholarship for the young man, then in his early twenties, so he could go to university.

And so Pascal left Mbuji Mayi again, studied at the Protestant University in Kisangani, and obtained a degree in theology. He came back to Mbuji Mayi in 1979 and was ordained as a pastor and given a congregation. He was assigned to Sangilayi Bipemba, the congregation that had trained and shaped him.

Pascal was soon drawn into various leadership roles in the CEM, and he served under both leadership factions. He also served as headmaster in the schools of the CEM. In this capacity, Pascal trained many people in the area of religion, particularly young people, who for the most part are faithful servants in the church today. In his own words, he became "someone to whom people came when they ran into problems."

---

photo—Pascal Misakayabo

During his time as a pastor he had frequent interactions with church leaders, while conflict among them continued to simmer. He attended all the steering committee meetings, even before he was appointed to the committee. He also dealt with the conflict as it played out in his own congregation, where tensions rose against another congregation in the city.

In 1993 Pastor Pascal Blaise Misakayabo made a decisive move. He assembled a number of fellow pastors whose sympathies, like his, were on one side. Together they accepted the leadership of the opposing faction. This finally brought the rival CEM groups together. In 1995, he was elected president and legal representative in the assembly led by the former opponent, and thus he moved into the top leadership position of the CEM.

In this capacity, he has to his credit several successful projects for the good of the CEM. But the most important is, he says, "having reconciled the members of the CEM—that is, having given the members of the CEM the desire to belong to a single body, the CEM." It's this unity that he left to the CEM at the close of his double term as head of the CEM (1995–2005).

In addition to his courageous acts of reconciliation, Pascal fought a great deal to ground the church on a properly religious foundation, in opposing the existence of a category of council members who were given permanent positions on the council. These council members, who were no longer elected by, or accountable to, their respective congregations, often reflected badly on the other faithful, acting far from the will of God and serving their own interests. He expresses his satisfaction on this subject, saying: "I am pleased to see those who succeeded me at the head of the CEM making this philosophy their own and wanting to give all the members of the CEM the same rights"—that is, to be represented by people of their choosing.

In his attempts to explain the meaning of this disorder that constantly threatened the cohesion of the CEM, Pascal notes: "The discrimination born of the creation of permanent council members is a consequence of the conditions in which the CEM was created: the crisis that preceded and followed the political independence of our nation. After being sent away from Ndjoko Punda, the members of the CIM (Congo Inland Mission) making up this wave were admitted and given responsibilities in the young church, with no account taken of their past. The first president of the CEM had no choice in doing this, because he was absolutely committed to his goal of setting up a new church. But it is the cause of the imbroglio in the CEM."

Pascal Blaise Misakayabo remains, with his wife and six children, attached to the CEM, where he serves God today as head of the CEM missionary district of Kinshasa. He constantly says: "The CEM is really and truly my religious assembly; nothing will be able to force me to leave it."

Jean Félix Chimbalanga

60 ❖ I'll spend the night in front of the door

Esther Mbombo wa Tshipongo was a strong and generous woman, whose dedication to the church sometimes made her an object of criticism and conflict. Someone who knew her says, "Her only response was to suppress her tears and devote herself to reconciliation, even if she wasn't at fault."

Many people remember Esther Mbombo, who passed away in 2006 at the age of seventy, because she was an influential figure in both the Evangelical Mennonite Church (CEM) and the ecumenical group Church of Christ in Congo (ECC).

She was brought up in a Presbyterian family in East Kasai and married Pierre Tshiamala. Shortly after their marriage they moved to Bujumbura, Burundi, where the first five of their nine children were born. They left Bujumbura in 1962 and moved back to Mbuji Mayi in the newly independent Congo.

In Mbuji Mayi Esther continued to attend a Presbyterian church until 1967, when the couple bought their own property. It happened to be near the first congregation, Sangilayi, of what is now the CEM.

Esther was intrigued by two things about the CEM. First, she had enrolled her children in the CEM secondary school, and she liked the daily worship services at the school. Second, she valued the Bible teachings of Pastor Mathieu Kazadi at the Sangilayi congregation, which she attended sometimes because her former church was far from her new home. She decided to become a member of Sangilayi and to be baptized according to Anabaptist practice. Esther was baptized, along with those of her children who had attained the age of reason, and she became an active member of the congregation.

Esther immediately joined the choir and amazed people not only with her singing prowess but also with the generosity of her service. She was a woman whose personal circumstances were difficult, but she took on responsibility for welcoming new people in church, often by presenting them with a chicken that she provided. The church authorities quickly gave her responsibility for congregational protocol. For several years Esther Mbombo attended to welcoming and seating people, cleaning the church, and taking care of children during services.

Several years later Esther Mbombo wa Tshipongo founded and directed a woman's chorale. This choir still exists five years after her death. When she was still young, she became president of the women of Sangilayi and then of all the CEM women of East Kasai. A woman of unshakable faith, she did her utmost to devote herself to the cause of women who came to her in time of trouble. In happy or sad developments, she was often the first to respond. She always made it a point to be present at gatherings, whether they were in town or far from town.

She was a fervent evangelist and advocate for Anabaptism. She brought a number of women to the church, including some former Presbyterians who recognized their affinity with Anabaptist teachings, thanks to Esther Mbombo's teaching. She sustained and encouraged the faith of her peers, telling them, "I exhort you, my children, you who have studied more than I, to dedicate yourselves to the service of the Lord, because it could happen, one never knows, that I could leave this place or leave this world."

All of this activity came at the price of some friction in her own household—with her husband, Pierre, his family members, and with other women. Because of the time she dedicated to the Lord's service, her frequent absences and late arrivals at home, some called her stupid or unfaithful. But Esther never conceded. She always said, "God is everything to me."

On one occasion she came home late at night after a mission. Some of her group decided to accompany her, in order to protect her from harassment by her husband. One of these women reports that Pierre had locked the door for the night and refused to talk to his wife or open the door for her. Esther kindly sent away her defenders, telling them, "If Pierre won't open up for me, I'll spend the night in front of the door."

Whatever worries, criticism, false accusations, and insults her husband, his family, and others subjected her to, Esther stayed firm and persuasive. Her faith radiated throughout the neighborhood, in the church, and in her household. To justify her comings and goings, she would retort to Pierre's relatives, "I do everything that is needed for the family. I feed you, I educate your children. Beyond everything that I do for the family, I have the duty to work for the Lord as well." She eventually led her husband to the church.

Esther was an indefatigable mobilizer of women. Her competence in leading women led to her elevation to the rank of vice president of the women of CEM. These new duties once again brought her the approval of the woman and confirmed her as a good Christian. She set herself to evangelizing and exhorting the women of East Kasai, reminding them that she would not be with them forever.

Esther Mbombo was preoccupied by the quest for peace in the heart of the CEM, as it was torn apart by leadership conflicts between Pastor Zacharie Nkumbi and Pastor André Ntumba. She tried in 1993 to reconcile the two. Although she was roughed up by partisans of the former when they invaded the church, Esther didn't hesitate to forgive her torturers during the reconciliation meetings organized by CEM in 1998 and 2006. She was a partisan of nonviolence and never gave evil for evil, whether in her official duties or her married life.

The authorities of the East Kasai Church of Christ in Congo (ECC) asked her to join and lead the Thousand Voices, an ecumenical chorale that brings together women from all Protestant groups. Her influence was so great that she is still remembered in all large church gatherings.

But Esther's greatest contribution to the ECC was a lesson of justice and truth, which unfortunately caused her biological brothers and sisters to reject her. One of her brothers was in a leadership conflict with the then-president of the East Kasai ECC which also involved the Presbyterian church. Because of this, her brothers demanded that she leave the Thousand Voices chorale. But she refused, saying, "If we really are Christians, we can never divide ourselves based on tribal differences."

Esther passed away in 2006. Benjamin Mubenga, president of CEM,[1] recalls how much she is still missed. Noticing that no food had been provided for participants in a recent denominational meeting, he declared, "This lack of food makes me think of Mbombo wa Tshipongo, who never spared the effort to mobilize women to provide food in such a situation."

Jean Félix Chimbalanga

1 See "Benjamin Mubenga's quest for peace and development" (chapter 73).

61 ⚜ A singer-songwriter's debt of gratitude

José Tshiakatumba's parents took him to a charismatic church in Mbuji Mayi when he was a child, and he found God there. But it was music that brought him to the Sangilayi congregation of the Evangelical Mennonite Church (CEM). When he was fifteen, in 1989, he was attracted to the songs performed by that congregation's World Revival Choir, Chorémon, and he become a member of the choir. "I sang as I had to sing for my Lord, " he says.

José soon became a composer for the choir. His first composition was "We are a people of our Lord Jesus"; his latest is "I adore you, Lord Jesus," which reminds Christians that there is only one master worthy of worship: "What Jesus has done in the world is visible. He is the only one to have been put to death and who rose from the dead, unlike all those who have claimed it before and after him."

The hymns he composed are a legacy of Chorémon and accompany the Sangilayi congregation's evangelistic outreach across the CEM. José's music ministry has brought other young people to Christ, including René Katombe, current president of the Sangilayi youth, who had Mennonite parents. For him, says José, "I am a role model in the world of music."

Besides serving as a singer-songwriter, José Tshiakatumba has also served his Lord as an evangelist, first for the Youth for Christ of CEM Sangilayi (1992), and then as assistant to the evangelist in

photo—José Tshiakatumba

the same congregation, from 2001 to this day. He himself was the speaker at one memorable three-day campaign that he organized at the Sangilayi congregation. New souls were won to Christ, including many who today are influential members of the congregation. José had the honor of having his parents and an uncle participate in this evangelistic campaign.

In addition, he served as provincial president of Youth for Christ of East Kasai from 2001 to 2003. He embarked on tours in several communities outside Mbuji Mayi to raise young people's awareness of Anabaptist doctrine and how they can support God's work. He moved to Kinshasa, capital of Congo, in 2003. Within days after joining the CEM Bumbu congregation in Kinshasa, José was named vice president of CEM youth in Kinshasa, a position he continues to exercise.

José Tshiakatumba is recognized as the initiator (in 2001) of morning devotions in Sangilayi: "It is because of a thirst for prayer that I was led to organize the prayer meeting that continues to be held in my congregation," he says.

José was baptized in 1994 at Sangilayi by Pastor Pascal Blaise Misakayabo.[1] A few years ago he married the pastor's youngest daughter, Annie Kanyanga, and they have a little girl.

"Recognizing Jesus as Lord and Savior is the first duty of every Christian," José says. "It is through this recognition that Jesus blessed my undertakings and gives me, in the proper measure, what I need." Because of this, José said he does not need to be repaid by the church for all he has done: "It's CEM and CEM Sangilayi who made it possible for me to find the way of salvation by training me and showing me who is my Savior." And so, he admits, "It is rather I who owe a debt to my congregation and to my community."

Jean Félix Chimbalanga

1 See "The desire to belong to one body" (chapter 59).

62 ❧ Bisonsa Bimpe, sorcerer's daughter

Three pastors found the young woman dancing on a tabletop. "They found me acting indecently and saying insane things, when they called me to them," says Bisonsa Bimpe. "I came down quickly from the tabletop where I was unabashedly dancing, still dancing as I responded to their call. As soon as I arrived at their level, they asked me to kneel, and they prayed for me. Right then, they told me to take them to my house, where they again prayed for me."

After this act of deliverance, the men involved, including Jean Marie Kanyinda, with whom Bisonsa was already acquainted because she had grown up with him, promised to come back the next day to take her to prayer meeting. And so they did. The servants of God, all Mennonites from the Evangelical Mennonite Church (CEM), came back to Bisonsa's house and took her to the morning prayer service organized at the house of Mama Tshilanda Musadi, member of the Kashala Bonzola congregation in Mbuji Mayi. The day after that they did the same and continued to do so until the time when they took her to a service at the church. It was, she says, a very odd conversion.

Bisonsa Bimpe was born in 1947. Her parents were great fetishists who didn't believe in God but instead believed in the power of spirits and spells. Her father, she says, was one of those who used that power: "Once they finger you, you die without any other form of trial." The farthest Bisonsa Bimpe went in school was her fifth year

photo—Bisonsa Bimpe

of primary education, which she was not able to finish because her father was made to retire; as a result his whole family had to move to Bena Kalenda, his native village.

An imposing woman, Bisonsa Bimpe was the object of much respect, as she had a lot of property. But curiously, her property began to dwindle progressively from the day she decided to consecrate her life to God, and especially when she began to attend church: "It seemed to me a chance for me to minimize myself and lower myself with regard to my attitudes and the crudeness of my language," she admits.

In 1972, three months after joining the Kashala Bonzola congregation, Bisonsa Bimpe was named a deaconess, and all of the parish finances were entrusted to her management. But she was not baptized until 1975, after having spent three years in the church. For four years, Bisonsa Bimpe performed without fail her duties as deaconess. She then served two years as vice president of the congregation's women's group, beginning in 1979. In that position, Bisonsa began to evangelize her delinquent friends in order to bring them to Christ. Today some of these women are still part of the church; some have abandoned the Anabaptist faith for the Catholic faith; and others have followed different leaders into different congregations. Similarly, she won many people to Christ at the city market, including Jacqueline Kalenga, currently national vice president of the Mennonite Women's Union.[1] Bisonsa evangelized her own family members, including a younger brother whom she helped when he was falsely accused of the murder of his friend, who was actually killed by bandits.

Named to the leadership council for the women of the Mbuji Mayi churches in 1982, Bisonsa Bimpe worked on settling differences in the homes of Christians as well as conflicts in the parishes, with the hope of procuring peace for all. However, her principal role was to exhort members of the leadership committee to live in peace and harmony and lead exemplary lives in order to bring their husbands to Christ if they weren't part of the church. Because of her fervor and commitment to the service of the Lord, Mama Bisonsa became vice president and then president of the Mbuji Mayi CEM women citywide, a post she held until 2009.

1 See "She saw CEM in a vision" (chapter 63).

Because of changes and conflicts in the CEM over the years, Bisonsa had begun to worship at a different CEM congregation. A few years later, she left this church over a disagreement with the pastor after a misunderstanding on the subject of a family in difficulty. At the invitation of her daughter, she began to attend another church, not part of CEM. After attending her daughter's church for three months, she had a vision of a man dressed in a white cassock, sitting in the vehicle in which she was riding. He said to her: "Come back to your first church and don't be angry, for a mother should not harbor endless anger." Because she didn't heed the message, a week later the same man appeared to her again, with the same message. She then returned to the CEM, attending a third congregation, where she has been for five years.

Bisonsa Bimpe grounds her faith and her discipleship on God's response to her prayers of intercession. She says, "All the difficult questions posed to me have been resolved by God after intercessory prayer addressed to him." As an example, Bisonsa cites the case of Romains Mbikayi and her children, whom God liberated from "wildness and barbarity." She affirms: "For all these problems, God answered my prayers and those of his servants, for all my children who were wild have calmed down. What's more, God has protected my life even though I was wealthy and lived a dirty life."

Today, Bisonsa Bimpe believes herself to be blessed, all the more so since her conversion and that of her brothers and sisters led to her father's conversion. Papa Nzolo converted to Christianity at an advanced age in 1996. He exclaimed: "What pleasure is there for me in not entrusting myself to God, if all my children have done so?" He passed away ten years later, having lived more than a hundred years.

Jean Félix Chimbalanga

63 ⁂ She saw CEM in a vision

Born in 1957 in Kolwezi, Jacqueline Kalenga Biayi (Jacquie, to her friends), came from a non-Christian family. She was married early to Musungayi Masanka, and from this union came six children, three of whom have passed away.

Jacqueline turned to God after the conversion of her husband, but before that she attended the Catholic church of Kolwezi, like all students attending Catholic schools. Not wanting to break an old habit, she attended Catholic worship in the morning and her husband's church in the evening. Jacqueline ended up belonging to a charismatic prayer group within her Catholic congregation.

After a relatively long period during which she attended neither her husband's church nor the prayer group, a vision appeared to her. In this vision Jacquie saw herself brought to a place where there was a church building. On the wall was inscribed the abbreviation "CEM." Asking a man at this place what the church building and the inscriptions on it meant, the man told her that this is the church where she should worship.

Encouraged by one of her friends, who believed that the vision indeed indicated the church where she should pray, Jacqueline had the conviction that the CEM—Evangelical Mennonite Church—was this church where she was called to serve God. As she never received any message contrary to this conviction, and as her home and many others were experiencing the torments of violence and ethnic intol-

photo—Jacqueline Biayi

erance, Jacqueline made every effort to believe that her church was CEM, even though she had never heard of such a church. When she was at the train station at Kolwezi, being forcibly expelled from her home, Jacqueline kept in her mind this amazing revelation that created in her the ardent desire to belong to CEM.

In 1993, six months after arriving at Mbuji Mayi, Jacqueline found herself in the market at Bakwa Dianga, where she sold secondhand clothes. Attracted by the hymns Jacquie was singing, a woman named Bisonsa Bimpe[1] approached her. When asked which church she belonged to, without hesitating Jacquie responded, "The CEM." She was astonished to learn that her visitor was also a member of CEM. Bisonsa gave her a Christian embrace and invited her to come pray at the CEM Ditekemena congregation. Bisonsa took responsibility to send people to show her the way. Mama Mbuyi, sent by Bisonsa Bimpe, missed Jacqueline the first time she went to find her. Mama Ngalula found her and made possible her first visit. As the result of the efforts of these three women, in June 1994 Jacqueline walked across the threshold of the Ditekemena congregation.

Jacqueline Kalenga attended the congregation alone. Her husband was suspicious. He wanted to become a member of a more permissive church, as he hoped to marry several wives.

Having twice been baptized, first with the Catholics by sprinkling and then in the prayer group at Kolwezi by immersion, Jacqueline was excused from a third baptism at CEM Ditekemena and became a member in a ceremony of reception.

In 1995 she lost her oldest daughter. Because of this difficult trial, she missed coming to the congregation for two weeks. After Elder Kabeya Dibwe and the entire congregation came to console her, she once again took up the path to the congregation.

There was a major incident in the congregation the very day that Jacqueline began to come back. It was the arrest of Kabangu Kasonga, pastor of Ditekemena, following the partisan tendencies displayed by himself and Mpoyi Odate after the 1995 General Council. This imbroglio within CEM and at Ditekemena greatly mortified Jacqueline Kalenga, to the point that she exclaimed, her self-respect wounded, "Where will I go to find peace? Everywhere, there is no longer peace: at the house there are torments, and at the church, conflicts."

---

1 See "Bisonsa Bimpe, sorcerer's daughter" (chapter 62).

The Ditekemena congregation exploded because of that conflict. After the congregation reconvened and then dispersed again in 1999 because of a serious generational conflict, Jacqueline decided finally to join the CEM Ditalala congregation.

From then on, although she held no particular office, Jacqueline Kalenga did all she could to console and encourage the church women to rapidly put into practice the decisions of the women's committee for the district of East Mbuji Mayi. In 2001 the leaders of Ditalala made her president of women of the congregation.

A tireless intercessor, Jacqueline is always present at her congregation each time that prayer or other activities are planned. Besides, since 2005 Jacqueline Kalenga serves CEM as vice president for all CEM women. Her availability to serve God has resulted in her receiving God's help in turn. His assistance, protection, and salvation have been powerful aids in her struggle against the misfortune and sicknesses that attack her. Once attacked by a powerful cough that made her lose her voice, she prayed to God and received a vision in which a man told her, "Do not regret that you suffer from this cough and that you have lost your voice, for this sickness would have progressed into tuberculosis without your prayers. But remember, this will never happen, and from now on you will no longer suffer from this."

Jacqueline has, as a peacemaker, worked for the reconciliation of spouses both outside and within her congregation. Outside the congregation she sought peace between two couples renting in the same housing unit as her own family.

Jacqueline has a strongly developed sense of forgiveness. She believes any insult must be forgiven after it has been admitted. Her example is an important and rare Christian quality. "I have often been disparaged by women in CEM who showed their displeasure because I was elevated to the position of women's secretary. These women asked themselves, without embarrassment in my presence, where I was when they were suffering pain for CEM's stability." In the face of these statements, she replied, "If the Lord himself had not recommended to me to pray at CEM, I would have gone elsewhere." Once this response was given, Jacqueline states, "All was erased, and when we saw each other the next day, life goes on as if nothing had happened."

Jacqueline says, "God is counting on me to serve him. No matter where one comes from, when one's star shines for the service of the Lord, it is good that the person truly puts herself at his service and that she is accepted by all."

Jean Félix Chimbalanga

64 ⚜ Felled by Ebola

Rodolphe Kasandji was born in Bandundu Province in 1945. Since boyhood he had been a gatherer of edible grubs (a great delicacy), a weaver of mats, and a carver of walking canes. His father died when he was young, but his mother remarried and her new husband adopted Rodolphe.

In 1962, Rodolphe finished his primary studies at the Mukedi mission station. In the exodus during the Mulele Jeunesse rebellion a few years later, he left his parents and went to live in the city of Kikwit. There he pursued veterinary studies and continued to associate with the Mennonites. He sang for the Lord in a men's choir, Voices of Angels. He married Régine Kakeziko, and they had six children.

Rodolphe Kasandji served for a time as a nurse but left that profession for veterinary service in the Protestant Agriculture Program at Kibolo. In the end, however, he returned to nursing and became an emergency care worker at the Kikwit General Hospital.

On May 6, 1995, the Centers for Disease Control in the United States was notified by health authorities and the US Embassy in (then) Zaire of an outbreak of a deadly viral fever in Kikwit. The World Health Organization and the CDC identified the virus as Ebola, a virus that moves quickly, causes intense suffering, and is fatal to most of its victims. Ebola first appeared in Zaire in 1976.

The quick onset of symptoms from the time the disease becomes contagious in an individual makes it easy to identify sick individuals

---

photo—Rodolphe Kasandji

and limits the spread of the disease. The outbreaks can be contained, and Ebola disappears from the scene for years at a time. Sadly, however, Ebola outbreaks occur most easily in hospitals where even basic sanitation is often a luxury, so many of the victims are hospital workers.

This was the case for Rodolphe Kasandji. He and two of his close friends caught the virus caring for their patients. Rudolphe passed away in October 1995.

Jackson Beleji

65 ⁂ Trust in the Lord and tell the truth

In 1959 Samuel Kakesa[1] married Françoise Kafutshi, who like Samuel grew up in a Christian family from the Mukedi mission station, although Françoise's family had moved around because her father worked in a large Belgian palm oil refinery. She had a solid but somewhat limited education. She was nevertheless well prepared to accompany her husband on his rise to church leadership. After he ended his work as legal representative, Mama Kafutshi was elevated in 1976 to the function of president of the women of the Mennonite Church of (then) Zaire.

She says she did not campaign for this position but was elected unanimously by the men and women of the church, under the inspiration of the Holy Spirit. For twelve years she succeeded in leading the women in an impeccable fashion, with a level of instruction fitting even for those better educated than she was. Trusting always in the Lord, Françoise had only one motto: "Tell the truth."

In accordance with John 8:22, she believes that the truth will set you free. But she emphasizes that for Christians of all confessions, the truth must not be considered a system or an ideology, and still less a philosophy, but must be identified as a person, Jesus Christ. For her, to betray the truth is not only a moral transgression but an apostasy, a denial of one's faith.

---

photo—Françoise Kafutshi (right) assists a sewing student

1 See "An open Bible at rebel headquarters" (chapter 30).

Unfortunately, she notes, the trouble between Christians is a result of the fact that many consider the truth an abstraction. It is in the name of this truth that Mama Françoise contributed greatly to the emancipation of Mennonite women, piercing the convention of thinking of women as good only for motherhood, inferior to men, and condemned to submit to the laws of men. Because Mama Françoise did not tolerate lies and intrigues, she was little appreciated by men who were hurt by the truth, so she eventually left the women's leadership position in order to serve the church in other ways, without hypocrisy.

Her life has not been easy. She lost a large part of her family—father, mother, three sisters, her only brother, her daughter, and two nieces—in quick succession. She says, "Words fail me to describe the suffering that I endured in the course of these events." But she concludes by saying she accepted everything the Lord sent her.

Today she continues to train Mennonite women in a nongovernment organization called Association of Rural Women for Development. She bitterly regrets the inordinate ambitions of men and women who no longer fear God and instead sacrifice the interests of the church to profit their own interests. She encourages women to persevere in prayer to save the church, which is in danger of disappearing because of the hypocrisy of those who divide the work of the Lord.

But in the end, this woman is a symbol of the awakening of the conscience of Mennonite women. During her administration at the head of the women, she taught a number of them that women have a great role to play in society, that they need to come out from under the antique notion that they are good only for childbearing, and that they should bring solid assistance to the household through work of all kinds.

Today, at seventy Françoise Kafutshi is a grandmother who continues to serve her church in the Lukolela congregation in Kikwit, where everyone recognizes her merits. Her ideas have released energies for women and men alike to take control not only in their own households but in the church as well. She continues to emphasize "the belt of truth buckled around your waist" (Eph. 6:14) against all forces, human and satanic.

Vincent Ndandula

66 ❖ A living example of repentance

André Kabasela was born to a good Mennonite family. His father is a pastor in the Evangelical Mennonite Church (CEM) and a director of schools. André entered secondary school in the CEM system but never finished successfully. At times a traveling salesman and then a diamond miner, André also became a family man. He is married to Marie Bienda, and they have six living children.

André was baptized as a young man of seventeen, but he says now that he hadn't really encountered Christ and committed his life to him. He continued to smoke and drink alcohol with his friends as he had before. Nevertheless, he often told his peers, "In spite of everything I'm doing with you, I am going to become a pastor sometime in my life." When he was feeling bad after getting high he often joked around by interpreting biblical passages for his friends in crazy ways.

Little by little, though, André left these sinful practices behind and lost the taste for smoking and drinking. He separated himself from his old friends. In effect, following the advice of his father but above all by his own will, he broke definitively with that group in 1992.

In 1998 he and several of his brothers and sisters formed a choral group and began to sing in church. An older brother was the group's composer. The group fell apart when the composer moved away from Mbuji Mayi.

---

photo—André Kabasela

Two years after the dissolution of the group, in 2004, André Kabasela was elected president of the youth of the Bupole congregation. The responsibilities given him, along with the need for the word of God that had taken hold in him, created in André the desire to serve God as a pastor and teacher of the word. It was when Elder Jean Baptiste Muluimba became head of the congregation that André revealed his thoughts about serving in the pulpit. He asked the pastor how that comes about. Elder Muluimba assured him that leading hymns, leading worship, and interpreting scripture would come to him easily enough when the time came.

Indeed, André learned the basics of leading hymns and worship in two days of apprenticeship, and two weeks of practice was nearly enough to lend him a real professionalism. As for teaching the word, Pastor Muluimba recommended that he study the syllabus of sermons the congregation kept in the pulpit. André pored over this document in the light of the Bible.

One day, when Pastor Muluimba and other congregational leaders were unavailable to lead the service, the pastor surprised André by asking him to preach that Sunday as well as lead worship. André pulled it off admirably, using as his text the story of the replacement of Elijah by Elisha. "Everybody's admiration of the message that I gave convinced me of my talents as a teacher of the word of God," he says.

André's greatest accomplishment at Bupole was to revive all the activities of the congregation that had collapsed or gone dormant. This accomplishment was a result of that very first sermon. With this teaching he exhorted the faithful to stand up and serve God, because in serving him one has everything, happiness and eternal life.

In April 2010 André was ordained as an elder of the church by Pastor Benjamin Mubenga, president of the CEM. And in July of that year he was named pastor of the Tshidiendela congregation. He says, "With this consecration and nomination I have seen my dreams come true and my desire to be a servant of God materialize."

Everywhere he goes and in every circumstance, he is always ready to do something for the Lord. For example, he went to his home village to mourn his paternal uncle. He learned there that one of his cousins had also died and was going to be buried without a sermon for the survivors, so he volunteered to preach.

André is convinced that the money he earned mining diamonds, although it was substantial, was not as valuable as his unstable and unpredictable earnings as a servant of God. Besides, he says, his brothers, who never used to give him money, now do so without being asked. He maintains, "My present life is peaceful, because the little I receive in working for the Lord is managed and spent in good faith."

Jean Félix Chimbalanga

67 ❧ My heart made me do it

Nobody knows for sure how old she is, but she is in her forties. Musawu has a mental disability.

She converted to God more than fifteen years ago. Before that she frequented a Neo-Apostolic church in Lubumbashi, where she lived with her parents. After she arrived in Mbuji Mayi, she became attached to the Evangelical Mennonite Church (CEM), which she joined during an evangelistic campaign.

The church was not entirely welcoming at first. She became the object of mockery and condescension by some of the former CEM members and especially young people. Despite this deplorable marginalization, Musawu remained attached to her congregation, braving all the humiliations of which she was a victim.

The fact that she was not given formal roles to play in the church did not prevent Sister Musawu from participating wholeheartedly. She attended all the organized meetings of the Sangilayi congregation, especially the women's gatherings. She joined church members in community encounters and in prayer meetings.

Shortly after her integration into Sangilayi, Musawu found her own ministry, which she began entirely on her own. She developed the habit of always being the first one to arrive at church on Sunday. She would sweep the floor, carry the benches from the parish house, and arrange them in the church. Asked how she came to do this, Musawu says with conviction, "My heart made me do it." She adds, "If I

photo—Mama Musawu

don't sweep the church and carry in the benches I don't feel right. I never want the place to be dirty." The day of the interview, at 4:00 in the afternoon, she was waiting for the end of a young people's meeting so she could take the benches back to the parish house.

Musawu now knows that many people of the congregation, including the pastor and elders, greatly value her services. They often give her money. On this day she had tied some money, which an elder had given her, into a corner of her wraparound skirt.

Sister Musawu affirms that she brought her mother into adherence with the CEM, although her mother continues to worship with the Neo-Apostolics. However, although Musawu is dependent on her mother for everything else, she categorically refuses to go to her mother's church. She says, "I love only the CEM, not just any church."

Now the congregation loves her as well. As one can easily see, Sister Musawu accomplishes her ministry voluntarily and regularly, to the great satisfaction of all the members.

Jean Félix Chimbalanga

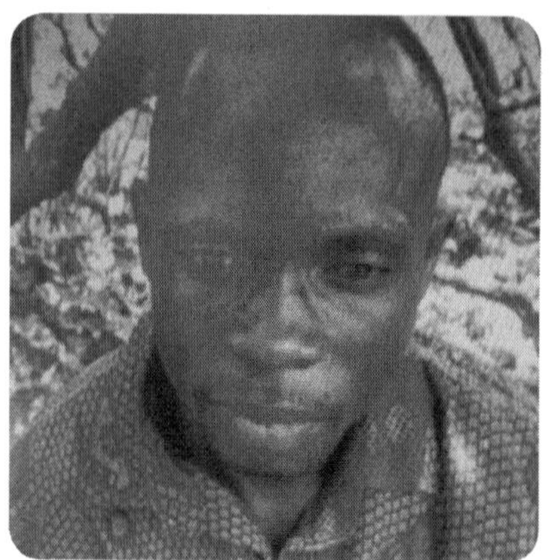

68 ✤ An explosive evangelist

Roger Tshilumba was drawn into the Evangelical Mennonite Church (CEM) Sangilayi Bipemba congregation by the music he heard one day in a choir rehearsal in 1983. The young high school student joined the choir and the church and was baptized in 1986. But the Christian life was not easy, at first, for this talented young man.

There was the problem with his maternal uncle, who had become Roger's guardian when he came to Mbuji Mayi to study. The uncle urged his nephew to leave the CEM Sangilayi, of which he had already become a member, to become part of "Animat," his own religion. Because of Roger's refusal to abandon what he already loved, he found himself in jail following a legal process initiated by the guardian.

The Sangilayi congregation interceded in his behalf and got him released after two days, at the price of a deposit. Because his relations with his uncle had disintegrated, the congregation took responsibility for getting him through school and helping him survive, providing rations when he needed them. He continued living with his uncle, sharing all of this with the household. Thanks to the support given to him by the church, Roger Tshilumba succeeded in finishing his secondary studies. At the same time he had the opportunity to take biblical training for planting new congregations.

---

photo—Roger Tshilumba

Then there was the matter of his marriage. He married a young woman from the congregation but left her, saying he found her "not submitted." He then married another woman in the congregation. Because of the complications, Roger was excommunicated. This pushed poor Roger into a remarkable state of church homelessness. Thus he found himself for a while with the Pentecostals and other groups. It was Pastor Benjamin Mubenga who finally helped him reconnect with the CEM where he remains to this day.

Throughout this youthful turmoil, however, Roger found ways to use his remarkable gifts to serve God. Pastor Célestin Kabengela,[1] with whom Roger works as an assistant pastor, declares, "In spite of the fact that he has an exaggerated dose of audacity which gives him the boldness to have no consideration for individuals superior to him, Roger Tshilumba remains until proven otherwise a powerful servant of God and a man with a great imagination for God's service."

Beginning in 1986, the young Tshilumba helped found an intercessors group in the Sangilayi congregation. The group prayed for the difficult times through which the congregation was passing and for the conflict that had shaken the CEM since 1975, which was on everybody's mind. Roger believes this intercession led to "the reconciliation in 1993 of the opposing parties."

But Roger Tshilumba's greatest contribution to the CEM has been bringing souls to Christ. "Evangelism, social outreach, intercession, and winning souls are very important roles I have played, given that the CEM is an evangelical community. The work that I have accomplished has its weight in gold and its real meaning."

As evangelist and social officer, Roger carried out many initiatives that proved to be productive in winning souls, first in Sangilayi and then in Inga, which he founded in collaboration with Célestin Kolela in 1993. Roger was among those who took charge of evangelistic mini-campaigns organized in the streets of Sangilayi, fifty to 200 converts at a time. In the same vein, while serving an interim pastorate in the Muindila congregation, Roger Tshilumba, in collaboration with the youth, initiated gatherings such as days of praise and marathon prayers, inviting particular individuals, most of whom ended up becoming members of Muindila.

Constantly using his gift for evangelism, he increased the numbers of the Dipumba congregation from thirty to 157, when he served

1 See "Saved from suicide by a vision" (chapter 70).

with Jean Richard Muteba in a 2006 interim. Six months later, still using his gift, Roger founded the Disanka congregation and the Musawula Evangelical Circle, after having constituted an evangelical group in the Bufuki congregation of Mwene Ditu, where he works to this day.

Outside the CEM, of which he is a member, Roger Tshilumba has served God in many ways in other churches, where he is often invited to preach, and in international Christian organizations. He has worked since 2009 as coordinator of Christian children's activities in Mwene Ditu for Children in Christ (CIC), whose goal is to teach the word of God to Christian children so they can teach it to other children. In CIC Roger has already trained twelve children, age eleven to fourteen, who are able to pray, sing for Christ, and preach the word of God. He says the children also become counselors in their families. One young girl, he says, was successful in reconciling her father and her mother, who had earlier lived "like dog and cat."

Roger declares: "I was not in the beginning a man of peace, but thanks to my membership in the CEM, which in its doctrine advocates peace, I have become a peacemaker." In fact, he successfully reconciled, as recently as 2010, members of his own family who had been in conflict for many years. He never stops saying, "It is God who chose me to use me for his work."

Jean Félix Chimbalanga

69 ✥ A wide-awake woman

Mimi Kanku was ordained in July 2012, the first woman to be ordained by the Evangelical Mennonite Church of Congo (CEM). This young mother of two was also one of the first Congolese Mennonite women to study theology. But Mimi believes that everything she does is the Lord's work.

She was born in 1981 to a Mennonite family in Kinshasa. In fact, the Righini congregation of the CEM leased its lot from her parents. She began attending Sunday school as a child and became active in the church and the choir.

It was her pastor, along with the president of the CEM women in Kinshasa, who strongly urged Mimi to study theology. Mimi was convinced that she should follow this discipline, even though it might not lead to a pastorate, as she hoped. But at the time she was already enrolled in the National Pedagogical University, majoring in commercial sciences. She did not immediately change her studies.

The year 2006 brought many changes into Mimi's life. She married Belarmain Ngalula, who was a member of the Bumbu CEM congregation in Kinshasa. Their first child was born. Mimi left her home church and began attending her husband's congregation. With all of this going on, Mimi received a scholarship to pursue theological studies and enrolled in the department of theology at the Christian University of Kinshasa. She had to manage the demands of being a

photo—Mimi Kanku

wife and mother, along with academic requirements and often very late scholarship payments.

At Bumbu, Mimi took charge of Sunday school and immediately joined the choir, which at the time was composed essentially of the pastor's children. She missed her home church and was dissatisfied with the weaknesses she found in the new one. She is not afraid to say these were the consequence of poor leadership on the part of pastors who distributed funds unfairly, as well as regional leaders who replaced pastors in an untimely fashion.

All those irregularities led Mimi to leave CEM in order to worship at her mother's church in another denomination, where she immediately became a choir member and an intercessor. And it is there that she felt called to the Lord's service. "In effect, it was because they came to my house to take me to a prayer service or to the choir that I felt called to be in service to the Lord as his disciple."

But her marriage to Belarmain obliged her to reintegrate into the Bumbu congregation, where she pursued service to God in the Sunday school, the choir, as an intercessor, and as an officer in the women's group.

Mimi declares that she has never encountered shadows in her life. "I have lived my whole life in the church." That is why she believes that everything she has done for the Lord has been important. "I am the one who organized the Sunday school and strengthened the choir. I was at women's conventions from time to time and took care to see that CEM women stood up for their point of view, like the other women. Without role models in the CEM, I forced myself to moderate certain events and to lead singing—if only to improve the image of the CEM."

Although she had always wanted to organize big conventions, Mimi never had the courage to try it. It was when she went to university that she had both the courage and the means to do it—with the goal of taking up a challenge on behalf of her community. "I always want to do better for my congregation and my church," she says. "My church never used to organize women's conventions. But I organized the very first one of its kind. The occasion was Women's Month and the theme was 'Woman, Wake Up!'"

That was the time Mimi made history by being the first Mennonite woman to preach at a CEM event. This moment was crucial for her, because for the first time she was in front of a microphone that echoed far from the congregation. On the same trajectory, Mimi organized and led seminars never before held in her congregation, to the great satisfaction of believers and unbelievers alike.

Mimi believes that the Lord gives total support for all her ministries past and future. One of the strongest testimonies of this, she says, is that her children have suffered all kinds of illness but have always recovered. "In all kinds of unhappiness that I have known as a woman, mother, and servant, and in all the joys that I have had, God alone is my help."

Jean Félix Chimbalanga

70 ✣ Saved from suicide by a vision

When he enrolled in the Mennonite school at Mutena in 1954, Célestin Kabengela was required to repeat fifth grade, even though he was already eighteen years old and had successfully finished fifth grade at the Catholic school he had attended until then.

It may have been because the Catholic and Protestant systems were incompatible. It may also have been because his new teachers saw potential in the young Célestin that he didn't see himself. Célestin wanted to be a furniture maker. The head of the Mennonite school thought he could be a preacher and teacher. Later, when Célestin wanted to enroll in a military academy and successfully passed the entrance exam, this mentor told him, "We did not send you to study so that finally you would go serve in public administration or in the army."

Célestin never regretted being held back and redirected, but he had difficulty finding his own way. He studied pedagogy and the Bible with the Mennonites in Mutena, Tshikapa, and Ndjoko Punda. He became a teacher.

Even though he had been a good student, Célestin Kabengela did not live peacefully. In his early years, tormented by what he calls "a life crowned with failures," he even decided to commit suicide. But one day in Tshikapa, while he was awake, the future servant of God had a vision: a bright light, he explains, blinded him, and the Lord Jesus appeared to him saying, "Don't give in to your thoughts. Ask me

---

photo—Célestin Kabengela

for all that you desire!" And he retorted, "I want to have intelligence and wisdom. I want to be happy."

This vision so greatly comforted Celestin that he really dedicated himself to the service of God in the will of the Lord. Although he had been baptized in 1954, he considers this vision his true conversion experience. After that he began to serve God as an evangelist and later a pastor, evangelist, school administrator, and church leader.

Speaking of the importance of his conversion and of his discipleship, Pastor Célestin Kabengela declares, "My conversion to God and my discipleship are two important roles that I had to enjoy in my life, because there is nothing more important than that."

Although the testing has continued throughout his life, Célestin Kabengela remains attached to God while showing proof of a strong faith in him.

During the post-independence conflicts in 1962, Célestin was among those who fled the Tshikapa area and returned to their native area in southern Kasai. There he joined the staff of the church that would become the Evangelical Mennonite Church, led by Mathieu Kazadi. Célestin Kabengela was assigned to be evangelist of the Tshiaba Lutulu congregation, then consecrated elder of the church. In 1972, he was ordained as a pastor.

The leadership conflict that shook the CEM was particularly hard on him. People loyal to the faction of Zacharie Nkumbi bribed police and had him arrested and jailed briefly in 1985. Ten years later he was one of three church leaders who were kidnapped in Kinshasa and held captive for four days and nights by members of the national security service—again, it is believed, at the instigation of Nkumbi. Célestin and his companions were able to survive, thanks to the efforts of Jean Bokeleale, national president of the Church of Christ in Congo; Pierre Marini, his assistant and current national president; and other persons of goodwill.

Bernadette, his wife, has been struck by blindness for nearly two decades. His non-Christian family, friends, and many people outside the church advised him to repudiate her; but because of his faith and the vow of fidelity taken before God and the church, he accepted the role of participating in her suffering.

In his various roles, Pastor Célestin has left a remarkable imprint on the church by training and ordaining many other pastors, including a number who left to join the Pentecostals and other groups, because of the lamentable conflicts in CEM.

One of his convictions, as he never ceased to affirm, is that "no one can claim to serve God if his Spirit is not with him."

Jean Félix Chimbalanga

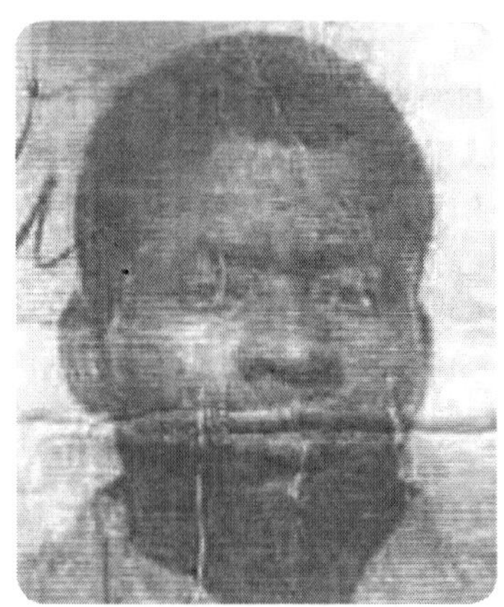

71 ⚘ Citizen of the heavenly kingdom

The testimonies collected from his wife and loved ones agree that what dominated the thinking of Pastor Dénis Mundela Tshibasu was seeking the kingdom of God. In a culture in which people prized their earthly nationality and tribal identities, he emphasized citizenship in the heavenly kingdom. He would always conclude by saying, "We should first seek the kingdom of God and his justice. All the rest will be given to us by him."

This man of strong spiritual conviction was born in 1942 in rural territory. He had the good fortune to be educated in Protestant schools of good reputation. He spent about five years in the Mutena primary school and completed pedagogical training in the same place. In that era, those coming out of pedagogical schools had a great advantage, and at the end of their studies many were immediately employed in primary teaching, which was well supported. For about ten years he carried out his beautiful profession with devotion and zeal.

Bit by bit, however, he felt within himself the birth of a pastoral vocation. He decided then to leave teaching to pursue a theological education. Unable to enroll in a theological seminary at the advanced level, he found his way to the Kalonda Bible Institute. During his four years of study he confirmed his vocation and was ordained in 1980.

With his wife, Victorine, he began a long pilgrimage in the Mennonite community, serving a number of congregations. A charitable,

---

photo—Dénis Mundela

tolerant, and peaceful man, he worked in perfect collaboration with other pastors, who sang praises of his exemplary behavior.

It is part of human nature, even among Christians, to want to dominate others. Many people serve others in order to gain the admiration of those around them. They may even congratulate themselves, in subtle pride, on being more spiritual than others. But Pastor Dénis left behind a great lesson for his church. The most important message to remember, he said, is that even these ways of dominating others are contrary to the laws of the kingdom of God. Before God, social ambition is not subject even to the law of survival of the fittest. Rather, the strong must look out for the weak.

With difficult working conditions, many servants of God have been weakened in their ministry. Despite superhuman efforts to continue his work, he gave his soul back to the Lord on February 3, 2009. The church remembers him fondly.

Vincent Ndandula

72 ⸙ We need Mama Treasurer more than the money

Thérèse Kamuanya married a Mennonite man, Gustave, the son of Pastor Onésime Mpoyi[1] of the Evangelical Mennonite Church (CEM) Kasekeyi congregation of Kabuela. This is how Thérèse, who grew up Catholic, came to the Evangelical Mennonite Church. After living for a brief time with Gustave's parents, Thérèse and Gustave left Kabuela for the city of Mbuji Mayi, where they had chosen to live.

Arriving in Mbuji Mayi, Thérèse and Gustave quickly became members of the CEM Bupole congregation. The welcome extended to her—and especially to her baby, Astrid—by the mothers of the congregation increased Thérèse's Anabaptist Christian faith and led her to become, without delay, a member of the Union of Mennonite Women of the Bupole congregation. "Throughout the seven years we stayed in Mbuji Mayi, in the Bupole congregation, I was a member of the mothers' federation and enthusiastically participated in all the meetings, on the second and the thirtieth of each month," she reports.

After Mbuji Mayi, Thérèse and her husband decided to move to Luputa, about 180 kilometers from Mbuji Mayi. There again the couple joined a CEM congregation, Munya wa Moyi. For the seven years they spent at Luputa, Thérèse joined with the women of the congregation and worked on their behalf.

1 See "A great pastor who turned the other cheek" (chapter 58).

As she gained knowledge and experience, Thérèse was sometimes designated to preach to the women. She proved to be a good preacher of the word of God. One day, the head of the Luputa CEM asked Thérèse to preach to her peers. She took her message from Proverbs 14:1 and spoke of a model woman. Because of this homily, the women affirmed Thérèse and asked her to serve as their president. But she did not accept the nomination, because she believed she was too young. Thérèse was a traditional woman.

In 1999, Thérèse and Gustave returned to Kabuela and rejoined their former congregation. Almost immediately, Thérèse Kamuanya was appointed secretary of the women's group. This time, despite her reluctance to take leadership, she accepted the role and exercised that function from 2000 to 2005. That year, documents report that her responsibilities were torn from her by the pastor at the time, following a land dispute that had set some of the members of the parish against the family of the late Pastor Onésime Mpoyi, her father-in-law.

Though she had been improperly discharged from office, Thérèse did not abandon the faith. She continued to meet with the women and participate in their projects. Her contributions to the group effort were still visible and revealed her genuine desire to contribute to the growth of her congregation. But she vowed never again to accept a position of responsibility in the church.

Her zeal and commitment to serve the Lord stem from her adherence to the advice her father-in-law gave her when she joined the family. "He told me, 'Whatever happens to you, do not give up the faith and do not leave the CEM. Use my example. It is my recommendation to you.'"

Eventually she was asked to return to her duties as secretary of the Kasekeyi women's group, and the documents confiscated from her were returned. For the sake of serving the Lord, Thérèse reversed her decision not to take leadership and agreed to continue her ministry within her congregation. She continues to serve to this day.

But it has not been easy. From time to time, for example, she has noted discrepancies between income and what the treasurer of the association declared. Faced with this situation, and in order not to shake the faith of that sister, she has urged the other sisters to overlook the problem. "We are in much greater need of Mama Treasurer than of what she keeps for the congregation," she tells them.

The mother of two boys and five girls, Thérèse has been a major contributor to the growth of CEM Kasekeyi in terms of community development and evangelism, through her participation in numerous projects, including working toward purchasing a sound system. Currently, however, Thérèse and the other women are struggling to get women's activities reinstated in Kasekeyi. These have been on hold for some time. Her efforts have focused on the meetings of mothers, collective work, and assistance to the needy.

Thérèse believes it is through her love of work, her ongoing concern to serve God, and the minimization of obstacles that present themselves that the Lord's grace and the hand of the eternal God accompany her in her life and in everything she does.

Jean Félix Chimbalanga

73 ❧Benjamin Mubenga's quest for peace and development

Benjamin Mubenga wa Kabanga is current president of the Evangelical Mennonite Church of Congo (CEM). He was born in Mbuji Mayi to Christian parents, though his mother and father each belonged to the church of their choice: his father to the Catholic church and his mother to the CEM.

His early education was also mixed. He did seven years of primary school with CEM and then finished at a Catholic school and continued his secondary education at Catholic schools. Benjamin's high school diploma was in science, the biology-chemistry track. Perhaps a poor Catholic student, Benjamin would opt for the CEM, the church of Georgette, his mother. Two factors would dictate young Benjamin's choice: the fact that he lived near the CEM congregation Dipumba Plaine, of which he is the pastor today, and his mother's habit of taking him where she went.

Benjamin Mubenga's conversion to God isn't easily separable from his entry into the Chorale Evangélique Butumbi bua Yepowa, his own creation. His membership in the choir, his membership in the Dipumba Plaine parish, and his attachment to God succeeded in convincing Pastor Zacharie Nkumbi of Benjamin's calling to serve the Lord and led to his receiving an educational scholarship for theology (1988). Benjamin married Béatrice Ndaya Tshishimbi in 1990. The Lord would bless their union with six sons and two daughters.

photo—Benjamin Mubenga and his wife, Beatrice Ndaya

After studies that he undertook with some difficulty because he was otherwise unemployed, Benjamin got a degree from what is now the Christian University of Kinshasa, followed by a theological graduate degree from the Protestant University of Congo. He then studied evangelism and church growth at the International Center for Evangelism. But the Mennonites who had fostered him seemed to have abandoned and forgotten him. Nevertheless, Mubenga founded a congregation in the sprawling outskirts of Kinshasa known as the Cité Mama Mobutu and put himself to work preaching the gospel of Jesus Christ from 1990 to 1995.

As a delegate to the General Council of the CEM in 1995, he had the opportunity to come back to Mbuji Mayi. He came back alone, leaving his wife and two children in miserable conditions and at high risk. Unable to return to Kinshasa—his family would eventually join him in Mbuji Mayi—Benjamin became a member of the Sangilayi Bipemba parish. Pastor Pascal Blaise Misakayabo[1] placed him at the head of its intercessory group. The effectiveness of Benjamin's work there led the pastor to name him assistant pastor. From that point on, he assumed as well the role of office director to Pastor Misakayabo, who was then the president of CEM.

In 1997, to his surprise, Benjamin was consecrated pastor at the end of the ordinary General Council held that year. He was named pastor of the Muindila parish in Mbuji Mayi, where he worked for several years. Moreover, he also worked as national director of the church's department of evangelism, missions, and Christian education (1995) and revolutionized a lot of things in the young people's meetings as well as in those of the adults. His warmth, commitment, and courage earned him the appointment of district head of the East Mbuji Mayi CEM.

These virtues of his are still apparent, and the leaders and faithful of the CEM grew in their trust for this servant of God, of whom they said: "Here's the man the CEM needs to rebuild itself in this time when nothing seems to be working."

When President Misakayabo was on one of his trips to the USA, in 2004, Pastor Benjamin seized his opportunity as interim leader to bravely resist his own Bakwanga tribal brothers, who had shamelessly, and with the complicity of certain authorities of the state, despoiled and already built on land where he had grown up: Dipum-

---

1 See "The desire to belong to one body" (chapter 59).

ba Plaine. Mobilizing men, women, and young people, Benjamin Mubenga fought with great energy to defend the lands of the CEM. He asked them to pledge with him that "whatever happens, the lands of Dipumba, Tshidiendela, and Bupole, the only physical heritage that today testifies to the visibility of the CEM, will never be taken from it, not one bit of them."

Benjamin won the battle over Dipumba Plaine, on which the encroachers had already built houses. Things would have happened similarly for Bupole, if it hadn't been for the noticeable complicity between the Bakwanga and certain members of the CEM. Meanwhile, the Tshidiendela case is still in the courts, where, it can be said, the CEM has the advantage.

With a view to achieving complete visibility for the CEM, Benjamin Mubenga, who was then national head of evangelism for the CEM, founded the Group of Mennonite Partners, which built and repaired church buildings, broadcast a religious program on Kasai Horizon Radio and Television, and carried out other initiatives. Basically, Benjamin gave a hand to all the lifeblood activities of the CEM, and the CEM became talked about.

In 2005, enjoying the growing trust of the faithful of the CEM, Benjamin was elected president/legal representative of the CEM, at the close of the General Council held in Dipumba Plaine.

Benjamin has since explained his vision for the flowering of the CEM, to return it to its place in the sun. His policy is to support others' talents, as he did with a number of individuals and young pastors. On mission to Kimande, in North Katanga Province, in his role of evangelist, Benjamin founded circles of CEM followers in this non-Mennonite area—a North Katanga mission field. He has brought a number of converts to the church, including his own brothers and sisters.

At the Church of Christ in the Congo, the ecumenical umbrella group where he is regional vice president under the Presbyterian Dieudonné Mbaya, Benjamin Mubenga is characterized by trenchant wisdom in the resolution of intra-community conflicts. Yet, because of certain excessive ambitions in certain of his collaborators looking to better position themselves, he is confronted with internal conflicts that are often unjustified.

In spite of all that, by pacifist and nonviolent means, he always seeks peace for his own denomination and for others as well. His pastoral style is to get out of the office and into the field. Taking no account of risks, he takes either a motorcycle or a vehicle to travel to faraway spots for pastoral visits and to follow the progress of various development projects for the CEM. Day or night, he never spares himself effort in going to the service of the Lord. His courage is clearly evident.

Jean Félix Chimbalanga

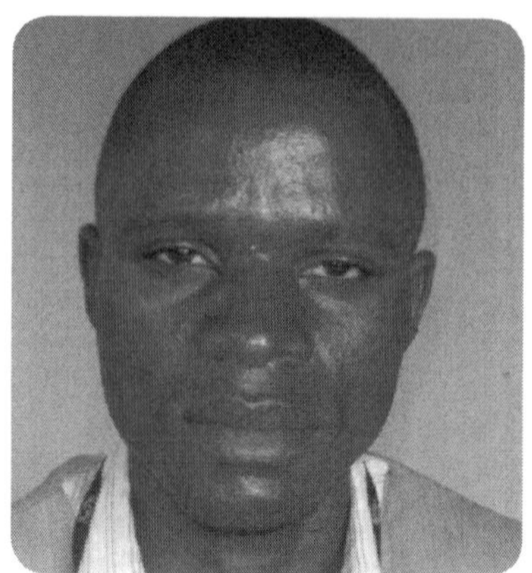

74 ꕥ Two children and a wedding

A wedding was taking place at the church near the home of five-year-old Jean Clairick Junior Lutumba in Mbuji Mayi. The little boy and his older sister, Marie, asked their parents for permission to attend this important occasion with the other children of the neighborhood. The parents agreed. It happened to be the wedding of Benjamin Mubenga and Béatrice Ndaya.[1] The church was the Dibumba Plaine congregation of the Evangelical Mennonite Church (CEM).

Years later, Mubenga would become national president of the CEM, and Jean Clairick would become national president of the CEM youth.

After that first visit to the church, the two children regularly attended church together. Their mother developed the habit of cleaning them up and sending them off to church with a few coins. These habits became permanent.

Several weeks or months later, the congregation set out to construct a church building, and each member agreed to bring a contribution in money or in kind. The commitment was underway. Jean Junior and his sister were taken by this need. They brought the news home and succeeded in getting their parents' permission—notably their mother's—to take bits of gravel and sand that Papa had piled up to build a wall around their family's lot. Every Sunday the young believers came with their contribution. Everybody was pleased by this

photo—Jean Clairick Junior Lutumba

1 See "Benjamin Mubenga's quest for peace and development" (chapter 73).

gesture from the two devoted children. The church leaders thought it necessary, however, to meet the parents.

The president of the women's group met Marie José, the children's mother, and brought her to Christ. Later, the spiritual path of Jean Junior and young Marie led progressively to the conversion of the whole family. Jean Junior was baptized in 2001, when he was sixteen. Just two years later he would become president of the congregation's youth, thanks to his intense involvement and his mastery of Anabaptist doctrine. For this, he recognizes the importance of a number of mentors in the church.

Jean Junior spread his wings as a youth leader—first in his congregation and then in the entire city of Mbuji Mayi. He created a theatrical troop to perform religious pieces such as "The Birth of Jesus" in theaters—with Junior often playing the role of Zechariah. He also worked to form choirs, collaborating with others who had more experience. His work was all for the purpose of leading young people to participate in the work of the Lord. He worked hard to unite and mobilize the youth of the ten congregations in Mbuji Mayi. One of his great contributions was a 2010 seminar to educate youth on HIV/AIDS.

His peers elected him national vice president of the CEM youth, and he became national president when his predecessor fell from grace. Throughout everything, his major concern has been that "the youth of CEM be well known throughout all the youth organizations and structures of our country as ardent workers for the Lord."

Although torn between academic demands and the demands of discipleship, Jean Clairick always gives precedence to the latter. He has been known to skip exams in order to attend church meetings. It is no different when it comes to work missions outside the country, such as one to Burkina Faso that he joined in October 2011.

Active, courageous, and a natural debater, Jean Clairick Junior never misses an opportunity to express his point of view, and he never fails to attract the sympathy of others. "I put the Lord's work first," he says, "because the Lord is the source of everything I do, even outside his ministry."

Jean Félix Chimbalanga

75 ❧ All I have to give is a daughter

In late summer of 1959 there was a flurry of activity at the Kandala mission station as young people from surrounding villages came to apply for entrance into the station schools for the coming year. One morning there was a tap at the veranda door of a local missionary. It was Pierre Khelendende, the lead pastor of the large station church.[1]

A portly man of medium height, Pastor Pierre had an innate gift for speaking. On the Sundays when it was his turn to preach in the station chapel, no one's attention drifted. His gift for oratory, his knowledge of scripture, and his firm grasp of the legends, proverbs, and idioms of his Pende people all made for sermons with an impact.

Beside Pastor Pierre stood a girl, his daughter, shyly looking down at the floor. She was dressed in a freshly ironed cotton print frock. Her skin shone from her early morning bath, and her hair was done up in neat little spikes. Her name was Léonie, the name she had adopted on the day of her baptism.

Invited into the missionary home, Pastor Pierre wasted no time in getting to the point. He explained that years ago he had met Jesus, and it had changed his whole life. He said that he and his wife had always longed for a son whom they could give back to the Lord for service in their beloved church. But the Lord had not seen fit to grant their request and had instead given them two daughters.

---

photo—Léonie Khelendende with her husband, Luadi Nari

1 See "A well-ordered pastor" (chapter 10).

Turning to the girl at his side, he said, "Léonie has never given us any trouble. She's been obedient and has been a great help to her mother. She finished primary school here at Kandala last spring with good grades. I still want to give a child to the Lord to his work." Pausing a moment, he continued: "Since I do not have a son, all I have to give is a daughter. Today I'm placing her in your hands. Treat her as you would your own child. Give her opportunity for further education and training. Let's see how the Lord can use her in his work and in our church. This is why I've come to you this morning."

A long moment of silence followed. While Léonie's eyes were averted, Pastor Pierre's gaze was fixed on the missionary, who was moved both by the deep yearning of the pastor and the audacity of his request. Girls and women had a low profile in the church. Their roles were still clearly defined: marriage, childbearing, and serving their families. Pastor Pierre's request reflected a startling readiness to push the African cultural envelope as well as to trust God to accept and use his daughter.

In the providence of God, that very fall the director of the four-year secondary school at Nyanga station had decided that it was time to take a historic step and admit a few bright girls into the entering class. One girl from the Banga station area had already been accepted, and the director was looking for a second qualified girl to be her classmate. When Léonie's school records were forwarded to him, the word soon came to Kandala that she had been accepted.

The first semester for the girls was not easy. Not only were studies at a challenging level, the girls were also teased by members of the overwhelming male majority of the class. "What are you doing here? Do you think girls are smart enough for this school? Didn't you understand that these courses are taught in French? Why aren't you married and doing what girls are supposed to do?"

The girls simply smiled, kept their peace, and studied hard.

Then came the first semester finals. When grades were made known, Léonie stood in the top 5 percent of the class. That put a stop to the boys' heckling.

Léonie became the first woman to graduate from the four-year high school program. She was one of the first women to be named director of a church primary school. To the delight of her parents, she was sent to her home station at Kandala, where she met and married a fellow Christian teacher, Luadi Nari.

Léonie accompanied her husband to Kinshasa when he was given a scholarship to enroll in a post-secondary pastoral training school. However, her request for a scholarship to enroll in the women's section of the same school was denied. Church leaders expressed regret but said they could not grant two scarce scholarships to the same family. The AIMM Women's Auxiliary in the US heard about her problem and granted her the funds she needed for the study program.

During three grueling years she carried on her studies with distinction, while caring for her children and providing nourishing meals for her family through careful use of their student rations.

Upon graduation, Léonie's husband was ordained to the ministry, but the Congo church was not yet ready to grant women this role. Léonie did not make an issue of this policy but simply made herself available at her husband's side. Her winsome smile, caring heart, and love for the Lord won her a large place in the Mennonite community of Kinshasa. Though not called "Rev. Léonie," she was, in fact and practice, precisely that.

Léonie died suddenly on a Christmas day, as she was making her way in a crowded city bus to her appointed place of ministry. Pastor Pierre's query had been fully answered. The Lord had indeed used their daughter in his service.

Jim Bertsche

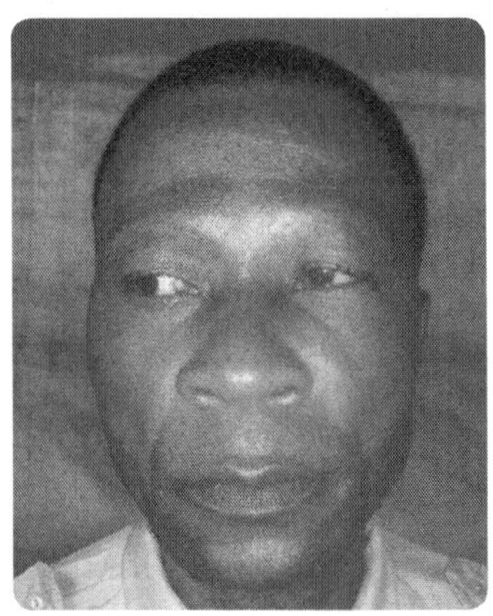

76 ❦ Sports, music, and prayer

In his fourth year at the Mfuti Institute, a large Catholic school of West Kasai, Jean Bosco Kabulo Kapudi was expelled because of his lack of discipline. The problem stemmed from the big head he admits he got from being a very good soccer player. It was a rough start on the path that would eventually lead him to become a Mennonite pastor in Kinshasa, and the whole journey would have its ups and downs.

Jean Bosco was eventually readmitted to the Mfuti Institute, after learning masonry at a trade school, and he got his education diploma in 1974. He promptly left for Kinshasa to join his older brothers, who wanted him to enroll in the Institute of Buildings and Public Works. But Jean Bosco was intent on becoming a great soccer player. He was recruited by the successful Motema Pembe club, but he soon left it because the club's fetishist practices clashed with his convictions and the advice of his father, who had told him, "To live well on this earth, one must want to have absolutely nothing to do with fetishes and have faith only in God, the sole protector."

The boxing match between George Foreman and Mohammed Ali took place on October 30, 1974, in Kinshasa. Although Jean Bosco didn't get to the match, afterward one of his cousins took him to a church where Foreman was visiting. When asked to speak by the young Protestants of the neighborhood, George Foreman declared, "Jesus Christ is Lord. He is the Savior of humanity and the transformer of the lives of those who believe in him." It was on this occa-

photo—Jean Bosco Kabulo

sion that Jean Bosco would become acquainted with a Protestant pastor, Papa Makanzu, who spoke to him about many things, including "serving the Lord in order to be saved."

Jean Bosco did become a mason and worked first with one of his brothers and then by himself. He abandoned that occupation a few years later—because, he says, he got tired of working for ungrateful clients. He then became a teacher and was hired to teach primary school in Kivuvu. The school belonged to a Protestant denomination, which required that he become a member of their church in order to get the job. Before joining that church, Jean Bosco could be found by turns with the Catholics, Jehovah's Witnesses, and at various Protestant churches.

In Kivuvu, Pastor Kasenda Mutombo took an interest in the young man, taking him into his congregation and making him its secretary, all the while introducing him to prayer and Bible reading. For this pastor, prayer was not the simple act of reciting words but the precious moment of speaking to God with great intelligence and attention. The pastor also assured Jean Bosco that "all the things that were done by Jesus and are written in the Bible are not fictions, but true things that really happened."

One day, after three days of prayer with the pastor, a great miracle occurred: the healing of a woman who had been bewitched by an evil spell cast by a rival. This healing gave Jean Bosco something to think about. He wondered if, in the name of Jesus, he too could perform healings. At the scene, seeing that he was stunned, the pastor said to him: "Jesus is alive. He healed this woman."

Jean Bosco remained with the pastor and would subsequently be made a deacon of his parish. Later a church dispute caused the pastor to leave the denomination. He invited Jean Bosco to stay in touch, even though the young man did not leave with him.

One day, Jean Bosco received a visit from a certain Constantin Mufuta, who had heard him sing, accompanied by colleagues. Mufuta, who was a member of the Evangelical Mennonite Church (CEM) congregation Ngiri Ngiri, asked him to start a choir. Jean Bosco accepted the request and began encouraging his friends to make music with Constantin Mufuta. But at the same time the authorities of the denomination where Jean Bosco still had his membership asked him to stay with the denomination and promised to make him a pastor.

Jean Bosco Kabulo rejected this idea out of hand, because he considered himself still too young and he was single. So he joined Mufuta at the Mennonite congregation and brought his fellow musicians with him. With a number of other young people from Ngiri Ngiri, Jean Bosco founded the choir called Messengers of the Cross.

For a while, the Messengers of the Cross performed hymns they collected from other groups, because they had no composers among them. Singing your own music is the mark of a prestigious choir. Feeling bad about this situation, Kabulo went to talk to his mentor, Kasende Mutombo, who judged the state of affairs unacceptable and believed that God could change it. He prayed for Jean Bosco, that he might become the composer of hymns for his group.

Upon his return to the congregation, Jean Bosco Kabulo announced to his friends: "From now on, you are supposed to count on me for the composition of hymns for our group. From now on, it will be out of the question to sing songs from groups other than ours." His friends made fun of him, not seeing how that could be possible. But he invited them to pray and meditate on this idea for three days.

Two days later, it was Constantin Mufuta who arrived with a song he had composed—"Goliath." He hummed it, and everyone accepted it. Four days later, Mufuta brought "God Created Me and He Gave Me Life." Two days later, he presented another song.

Every week from then on the group produced new songs, because Jean Bosco himself and another musician joined the team of composers. The choir was powerful and glorious. But because of tensions between the choir and the pastor of the church and its members, the choir would rebel against the congregation and become independent of the Ngiri Ngiri CEM. This move was against the will of Jean Bosco, but he nevertheless left the CEM for a while during the imbroglio. Eventually he came back as a result of the pleading of a number of the faithful.

Upon his return, things were not easy for him, because most of the members still did not trust him. But he held on, organizing choir and an intercessory group. He was named congregational evangelist and undertook a lot of work to reenergize the Bumbu parish in Kinshasa.

Eventually Jean Bosco received the charge to lead the Bumbu congregation as pastor. He is also the author of several initiatives that gave the CEM congregation Nouvelle Vision the acceptable status of a local church. His life is full of lessons in God's grace.

Jean Félix Chimbalanga

77 ❧ A virtuous woman

The life of Elisabeth Nzuji bears witness to God's sovereignty, to God's power to reveal himself in many people without regard to gender, race, profession, or origin. This revelation is a grace that he bestows on every person: to know him deeply and intimately and to experience his glory in all of life.

Born in Kitanda in 1943, Mama Elizabeth was married to Elie Kitambala. Of their five children, two became pastors, two married pastors, and the other became a doctor. Elizabeth was known as a woman who loved Christ and as a faithful wife, hardworking and kind to everyone in her household, until her sudden death in 1993.

She was a fervent choir member all her life. She loved to praise, adore, and thank God for his goodness and love through hymns, which she considered great prayers to God as well as acts of grace for her own life.

Despite her modest means, she contributed to the construction of the church through regular offerings. She participated effectively in acts of charity that the women organized within the congregation, such as aid to widows, orphans, prisoners, and the sick. She also showed abundant generosity to strangers and visitors.

She was a true aide to her husband, a medical worker who was constantly being transferred. Elizabeth's presence brought him stability and moral balance in this difficult task he performed for society. She contributed to honoring her husband through her actions,

---

photo—Elizabeth Nzuji

which are responsible for the fact that he is to this day a devout Christian. She raised her children in the fear of the Lord, and they in turn became a great source of blessing and pride for the family.

Elizabeth was sweet and calm. It was next to impossible to catch her using inappropriate or strong language in front of her relatives and husband. She was a good counselor to other women, young and old. She would fit the description of the virtuous woman of Proverbs 31.

Elizabeth's physical beauty did not leave men indifferent. The witness of her husband and church sisters take note of her victory over seduction, which Elizabeth displayed at various moments throughout her marriage. For example, after several transfers the couple arrived in the Belo sector of Idiofa territory, where Elie Kitambala became a public health agent. There a local priest tried to cause Elizabeth to fall into Satan's trap. She was able to resist this temptation and even to denounce her tormentor to her husband. After that, the priest did his best to disrupt the couple's marriage and have them evicted from the post under the pretext that they did not belong to the Catholic religion.

Despite all these vicissitudes, Elizabeth and her husband held firm in their marriage with love and fidelity until death separated them. She owed that strength of character to Mennonite doctrine and her determination to be always in service to the Lord. It was a lesson she left to other women.

Thus is manifest the hidden power of God in the individual. This power gives us peace in days of torment and distress. It makes us light in a world invaded by shadows. It also makes us victorious in a world full of failure, deception, and bitterness. This grace is the person of Jesus Christ, only Son of God.

May the Eternal raise up in our society such steadfast, virtuous women as Mama Elizabeth Nzuji to serve as examples for others.

Jackson Beleji

78 ⚜ A rich man in the Lord's service

Macaire Kilambo was born into a Mennonite family in 1961. From childhood he was a compliant boy, devoted to his parents and respectful. They passed on to him a good education and good moral conduct. He was baptized in the Mennonite Church of Congo (CMCo) in Gungu in 1987.

After studying in Mennonite primary and secondary schools, he gained a state diploma at the technical institute of agriculture and veterinary studies in Gungu. He married Wivine, and they have one child so far.

Macaire Kilambo is a successful merchant, but he has arrived at his current level of commerce with struggle and difficulty. He began by traveling long distances on foot from his native village to Tshikapa, carrying goods—hot peppers and other produce— on his head to sell at his destination. Through these sales he had God's blessing in obtaining capital, which encouraged him to abandon the sale of produce and turn to selling cattle. Currently he is the head of the KKM business based in Kikwit.

Macaire Kilambo does not fail to thank God for blessing him. The Bible tells us that everything comes from God. If you share your joy with others, the Eternal will bless you even more. This is the typical example of the one who abandons himself to the hands of God. In fact, as Kilambo says, "wealth must not separate us from God or his works. Rather we must recognize that whatever comes from the

---

photo—Macaire Kilambo with his wife Wivine Kilambo

hands of Christ no one can take away, and the Lord will see that it lasts a long time." Thus, he adds, "I am in service to people and I must continue to help people."

At the denomination level he has worked as a delegate to all the large assemblies. He has reconciled pastors in conflict several times. He has brought peace throughout the church province of North Bandundu. Because of his contribution in the resolution of conflicts God has elevated him to the rank of universal ambassador of peace.

He confirms his new career of universal ambassador of peace in his deeds in the church and elsewhere. In the Lukolela congregregation, where he worships, he built a large permanent building, bringing masons from Kinshasa to Kikwit and supporting them at his own expense. He has always made his resources available to the church. Kilambo has often helped delegates with transportation to get to the assemblies. Recently he put his large vehicle at the denomination's disposal for transporting material from Kinshasa to Tshikapa for constructing the Centennial Guest House. He helps anyone who approaches him—those with physical disabilities, widows, and orphans.

Although he had obligations in Kinshasa at the time, Macaire Kilambo abandoned his work to be present at the ordination of his wife as deaconess. If any other needs arise in the entire CMCo, he is available to lend his aid, because his desire is to see the church grow. He and all his family dedicate themselves body and soul to the Lord's service.

Jackson Beleji

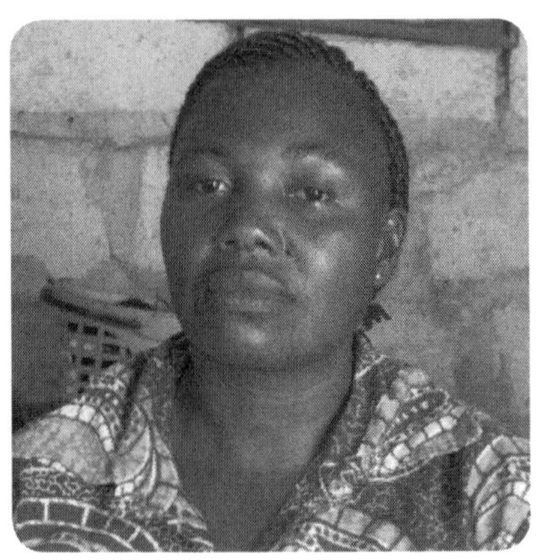

79 ✥ Annie Mbuyi's quest for peace

Annie Mbuyi's husband, Mathieu Shimatu, is the current vice president of Evangelical Mennonite Church (CEM). Throughout their life together she has found ways both to support his ministry and to develop her own gifts.

It began before they were married. They met when they were both singers in a church in the territory of Ngandajika. Annie's father was a deacon in the church, and Mathieu's older brother was president of the choir. They became engaged, and Mathieu left for Mbuji Mayi. Annie followed him and they were married. Mathieu had by then joined the CEM but Annie did not immediately break with the church of which they had been a part. In 1987, however, the young married woman was recruited into the church by an elder of the CEM Tshiala congregation, where her husband was already a member. "It was by submission to my husband that I finally became a member of CEM," she says.

Although she had been baptized in her previous church by immersion, she decided to be baptized a second time at CEM Tshiala. There she began to serve as an intercessor, a ministry she continues to this day in her current congregation, Bitabe, in Kinshasa.

While praying generally for everybody in the CEM and elsewhere, Annie Mbuyi prays incessantly for her husband, who works at CEM headquarters in Mbuji Mayi, far from Kinshasa, where the couple maintains their home and reared their seven children. Ac-

---

photo—Annie Mbuyi

cording to Annie, Mathieu's work is fraught with difficulties and conflicts. She recognizes that God answers her prayers by protecting her husband during the eight, nine, or ten months a year he spends away from their home.

A fervent evangelist herself, Annie has brought many people to the Lord and has helped stabilize numerous households that were subject to tensions. The beneficiaries of her services testify that without her interventions their marriages would have broken up. Annie heaps advice on those concerned, notably on women, whom she asks to be patient and not to follow the counsel of other women who don't tend to their own marriages. Out of respect she calls her husband "Papa Mathieu."

When Mathieu was a theology student at the Christian University of Kinshasa, Annie Mbuyi was trained as a seamstress, although she never really took to that profession. Nevertheless she made and sold small articles and food products to subsidize her husband's studies. She still does this to contribute to household support.

Attentive to the gift of sharing, Deaconess Annie receives with a joyful heart all who come to her home. She considers older people her brothers and sisters and those her children's age as her own children, offering them her care without discrimination. Her generosity has attracted many people to her. In turn, she has directed them toward CEM, where they become members.

Filled with love for the church, Annie worries about the negative attitudes of some pastors toward the church's rules and bylaws. "I am often pained when I learn there are squabbles between one pastor and another," she says. "My sadness is very great when that affects the church and members of little faith lose their faith in God." In the face of such problems, she sometimes takes courage to approach the servants of God concerned, asking them to review their behavior and live like ministers of God. Her most ardent concern, she says, is that the CEM find peace—that the church be in peace like other denominations in order to progress in the same way.

Annie testifies that she feels the hand of the Eternal sustaining her life. "I am alive," she says, "and at forty-five years of age, God has already made me a grandmother."

Jean Félix Chimbalanga

80 ⚘ A messenger of ecumenism

Dénis Mahouma has rendered forty years of faithful service as a registered nurse in a Catholic hospital. At the same time he has been an active lay leader in the Mennonite church in Kikwit. His life attests to his belief that Jesus Christ has broken all boundaries.

Born in 1948, Dénis was baptized at the age of eleven and completed his primary education at Kamayala in 1962. After two years of middle school at Kalonda, he enrolled in the medical institute at Kajiji and became a nurse. A brilliant, hard-working young man, he was immediately hired by the Catholic nuns of the congregation Notre Dame of the Faithful. He has served in their hospital ever since.

Married in 1972 to Evelyn, he and his wife have four sons and four daughters whom they have raised successfully, thanks to Dénis's steady employment.

This man of exemplary conduct has never hidden his membership in a Protestant church from the nuns with whom he works. Every Sunday he is in church, where he takes great responsibility as lay president. He has assumed, by turns, the duties of secretary of his local church council and chaplain of the Voices of Angels choir, of which he was one of the founders.

Ordained deacon in 1987 and elder in 1989, Dénis Mahouma is also president of the Mennonite Farmers of Kikwit. But this man of unparalleled humility knows how to manage his time so that he is always ready to respond to the call of his church community. De-

---

photo—Dénis Mahouma

spite the demands of his profession, he has greatly contributed to the birth of a Mennonite Church of Congo (CMCo) congregation in Misengi. He has supported out of his own pocket numerous expenses tied to the construction of the building.

Dénis and his wife have often hosted missionaries and Mennonite Central Committee volunteers in their home. They have taught the newcomers Kikongo, one of four national languages, which is spoken primarily in Bandundu Province.

Dénis has never experienced the least conflict between his service with the Catholics and his service to his own church. About holy communion, Dénis Mahouma says that he is happier to serve than to be served.

A peacemaker, he refuses to define the church of Christ in tribal terms. For him, Jesus Christ has broken all the ethno-tribal frontiers. He maintains that membership in the church of Christ should be our common denominator.

Vincent Ndandula

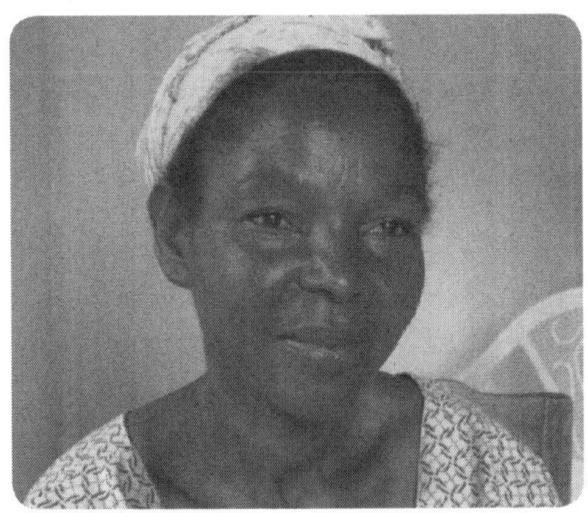

81 ❧ What if God visited my church and didn't find me?

Since the 1980s, Yvette Tshidibi has been a teacher of technical courses at the Kazadi High School of the Evangelical Mennonite Church (CEM) in Mbuji Mayi. But she did not become a member of the church in order to get the job. Rather, she believes God called her to the school, knowing that eventually she would be serving him in the church community.

In her youth, Yvette followed her parents to the Catholic church, in which they were fervent, practicing believers. She has a four-year degree in sewing from a Protestant secondary school. She has been divorced and has seven children with more than one husband.

It was in 2000 that Mama Yvette Tshidibi was first counted in the membership statistics of the Ditalala CEM congregation. "I truly encountered God at the Ditalala CEM because of the teachings of my pastors and elders of the church, who gave me peace, because before that I was a restless, unruly woman, dissatisfied in life and nervous."

After encountering God, Yvette affirms having gone to him and been heard by him: "I've been worshiping for ten years in Ditalala. Here, more than elsewhere, I understood that God listens to me, because he saved my year-and-a-half-old son after a serious and violent illness that the doctors of this world didn't succeed in treating."

At the church she ministers through intercessory prayer and as a leader of women. Yvette was named president of the women's

photo—Yvette Tshidibi

group in 2007. Her role consists of exhorting the women to behave in a way worthy of Christian women, and breaking up cliques in the interest of community service to the Lord. "Thanks to this exhortation, all the sin born of envy, disdain, and denigration has ceased, and all of us have peace in our parish," she says.

Preaching by example is important to Yvette, so she actively participates in all acts of service organized in her parish. "My participation in the work of God has awakened many people, especially the women, and pushed them to serve God as I do."

A tireless intercessor, Yvette Tshidibi has many proofs of the intervention of God in the many cases she has submitted to him: "The peace of heart that I have is something of great importance that I have gained in my Christian life." She adds, "When I pray for something with which to serve him, I receive an answer promptly and miraculously." One time she was hoping to participate in a training seminar on Christian education. Participants were expected to contribute to the costs of running the seminar. The Lord's help came to her when she had barely finished praying, only a few hours before the beginning of the seminar. A woman brought Yvette an order for children's clothes to be sewn. The money was enough to cover her contribution to the seminar as well as her transportation.

Yvette has offered her services to other local churches, Protestant and Catholic, as the residents of her neighborhood have found her to be a level-headed Christian. The Saints of Salvation church has gone so far as to propose that Yvette stay with them. But she has never accepted, believing that her place is at the CEM. She laughingly tells them, "If you keep me here, what would happen if God visited the CEM and didn't find me there?"

Jean Félix Chimbalanga

82 ❧ Together, pushing Mennonite boundaries

The Rev. Placide Yongo acknowledges that his task is not easy. He is a pastor in charge of "military morale," a chaplain to members of the military who are part of several congregations in Tshikapa. He himself is a captain in the army. This is a highly unusual position for a Mennonite pastor in the Congo, as it would be in North America.

"We counsel and encourage members of the military," he says. "Encouraging a conscience in military personnel—helping them want to do good and avoid evil—is a task that requires a lot of care." He believes his apostolic calling is comparable to that of servants of God who bring unbelievers to a recognition of God as the sole creator of the universe.

Placide Yongo was born in Mukedi in 1939 and baptized at the Mennonite mission on December 28, 1952. He attended primary school at the same place, high school at Nyanga, and finally trained at the Protestant theological school of Kinshasa from 1969 to 1973, followed by eight months of teacher training in Kikwit. He taught for six years and worked for twelve years as head of the Mukedi primary schools. He then joined the military and served first as a provincial chaplain for seven years in Bas-Congo.

Placide Yongo and Florentine Madiwasa married in 1961 and have now been married more than fifty years. Mama Madiwasa was born near Kahemba in 1942, went to primary school in Mukedi, and

photos—Florentine Madiwasa (left); Rev. Placide Yongo (right) was baptized at the mission in 1957. Before marriage, Florentine had had a year of training at the school of home economics, and she was one of eighteen women chosen in Ndjoko Punda for training and leadership in the movement to transfer leadership to Congolese. She was then trained in theology at the school for women in Kinshasa. When she was in her second year, she taught the first-year students.

In Tshikapa, Florentine was elected director of the Deaconess House where she would work for seven years; two skilled women assisted her with the heavy work, embroidery, dyeing, and sewing attractive men's and women's clothing. However, once the couple went into the army, Pastor Yongo says the deaconess house went downhill, and "today no one mentions it anymore."

The Yongos have eight children, four girls and four boys. All are well educated, some with the equivalent of a master's degree. "As for me, I am a military parent, the war is not our problem"—meaning that, although he is in the military system, war is not what he is about.

Both Placide and Florentine hope to set an example of the kind of life to be followed in the Christian community, dedicating themselves to their vocations in order to have the blessing of God and to find peace and blessing during their earthly lives as well as in the paradise to come. Their children, who have followed the counsel of their parents, are all appreciated in the environments where they work.

Jackson Beleji

83 ❧ A servant of God finds her gifts

Esther Misenga was born in 1987 in Mbuji Mayi, the oldest daughter in a family of seven children. She did her secondary studies in a pedagogical institute of the Evangelical Mennonite Church (CEM) but failed twice to pass the state exams at the end of her sixth year. That was the end of her studies, because her parents didn't have the means to allow her to repeat the year.

Did the fact that she was a member of two church choirs have something to do with her failure to pass the exam? Esther was baptized in 2001, at the age of fourteen, and the same year joined the Works of God choir. As if that wasn't enough, in 2003 she also became a member of the Sangilayi Bipemba congregation's choir, Chosabi. She never missed practices and services. One choir rehearsed every Tuesday, Thursday, and Saturday at 4:00. The other met on Monday, Thursday, and Saturday at 5:00.

But Esther doesn't link her double exam failure to her heavy choir schedule. "I still had plenty of time to dedicate to my studies," she says. "I can't say that I failed in my studies because of my responsibilities as a singer for the Lord."

In 2007, Esther became president of the Works of God choir, which brought sensitive responsibilities. She leaned on God for support in such things as acquiring and learning new songs and in counseling the group. She encouraged her peers to engage in service to the Lord, because "gaining the reward for what you do for the Lord is

---

photo—Esther Misenga

up to you and not anyone else." She continues, "This reward is eternal life, which is precious for every child of God."

In the same spirit, Esther dispenses moral advice to her charges—to respect each other, and to do your best in everything you do. She works constantly to mend relationships among the group members when the inevitable clashes erupt among the young people.

In her words of encouragement, Esther maintains that "the recompense, eternal life, comes in assenting to serve God according to the gift that everyone has received from his Holy Spirit." She believes that this reward is earthly as well as heavenly.

Esther's perseverance and faithfulness to God is manifest in her resistance to her father's pressure to leave the CEM Sangilayi church and its activities. Her father left for personal reasons and wanted her to leave as well. But she insisted on staying true to her commitment to participate regularly in rehearsals, concerts, worship services, and other congregational meetings. One of her brothers has also tried, unsuccessfully, to dislodge her from the congregation.

Despite these differences, Esther says her family "rejoices to see me honor and fear God, unlike other young women my age who aren't obedient to their parents and who take pleasure in the ways of the world." Esther has been a reconciler in her father's family. She recounts: "One of my aunts has had a grudge against her brothers, including my father. One day she came to our house and started to complain to me about her differences with her brothers. Without hesitating, I talked to her about the will of God in situations where one has been hurt by another. She was pacified by the words of the Bible, 'Do not render evil for evil.' My aunt immediately renounced her plans to set herself in conflict with her brothers."

Esther also serves the Lord as an intercessor in the congregation. She testifies that this new ministry interests her as much as the choir ministry, and she has thrown herself into it wholeheartedly. She says, "The Lord whom I serve knows me and sustains me in my social life as well as my spiritual life. He has saved me in difficult situations and serious illnesses. God takes care of me and protects me from the vicissitudes of this world." She has been tormented repeatedly by malaria. In 2006, for example, it brought on convulsions and she collapsed in church. But by the grace of God, she testifies, "my life was saved."

Another church member testifies to Esther's effectiveness as an intercessor. A mother brought a sick baby for prayer. Esther prayed for three days, and the mother prayed as well. The baby was healed.

The Sangilayi congregation rejoices to have Esther as a member and as a servant of Christ in its midst.

Jean Félix Chimbalanga

84 ❧ Simon Tshiombe, teacher turned chief

Born in 1936, Simon Tshiombe was the son of a prominent regional chief, but he chose to become a teacher. By 1952, at age sixteen, he had completed elementary school in Mutena as well as studies at the pedagogical school, and he was qualified as an elementary school teacher. He began a successful teaching career and married Ruth Dingeya in 1957. They had a peaceful family life with their twelve children. In that era teachers had sufficient means to raise any number of children.

As a teacher Simon never conducted himself as a master of events nor as a master of his pupils. Rather, he learned to listen to others, to dialogue with them. Together they learned to build a future as yet undefined.

But in 1984 events would take a different turn. Simon's father, the chief Kasonga wa Bena Lunda, had just died. It was necessary to find a successor to head the chiefdom. The family council decided to call on his son Simon. Unless he wanted to become alienated from his people, he had no choice but to bow to the will of his family and his tribe. Will there be, in the future, a way out in a situation of this kind? In Congolese society, the requirements of the village, the spirit of the ancestors, and traditions such as initiation rites must still be respected at all cost.

---

photo—Simon Tshiombe (left) with his father, Chief Kasonga

Thus began for Simon another type of life. Enthroned as traditional chief of the region, replacing his late father, he did not forget the commitments he had made at the time of his baptism. On that day he said to the Lord, "I have given up everything to follow you." He spent time meditating on the word of God and practiced it in his everyday life. He helped the church in his region to build churches and schools. Torn between the requirements of traditional power and Christian morality, he forced himself to preserve the values of Christianity in his family and among the population he governed.

Simon Tshiombe was struck by an illness that weakened and nearly paralyzed him, and he died in 2004. In spite of traditional requirements, the church organized a Christian funeral for him and opposed traditional practices that accompany the death of those who have assumed responsibilities of this kind. He had acted in his work in accord with the words of Christ to Peter, "Be shepherds of God's flock that is under your care, watching over them—not because you must, but because you are willing, as God wants you to be; not pursuing dishonest gain, but eager to serve; not lording it over those entrusted to you, but being examples to the flock" (1 Pet. 5:2–3; NIV).

Vincent Ndandula

85 ❧ All the arrows of the devil

François Mbuyi saw that the pastor of the Evangelical Mennonite Church (CEM) Kasekeyi congregation in Kabuela needed help. François at twenty-five had just landed in Kabuela. He had been a member of the Presbyterian community in his home territory, Katanda. When he was looking for a church home in Kabuela, the charismatic churches didn't appeal to him. "The doctrine and rites did not please me at all," he says. So, without being evangelized by anyone, he decided in 1996 to become a member of the CEM Kasekeyi congregation, who welcomed and included the young man.

François offered his services as a hymn leader, preacher, and intercessor. After getting agreement in principle from Pastor Tshiakatumba,[1] François became totally involved in serving God in these ministries. He turned out to be such a good preacher that the pulpit was occasionally handed over to him both at midweek meetings and during Sunday worship. Many old and new believers were strengthened in their faith in Christ by the teachings given by this young servant of God, who quickly earned a good reputation in the congregation.

In addition to these ministries, François Mbuyi was elected secretary of the Kasekeyi congregation, charged with recording all parish decisions taken at meetings of congregational councils, with maintaining the group's statistics, and with managing all the fi-

photo—François Mbuyi

1 See "A great pastor who turned the other cheek" (chapter 58).

nances and assets. His call to exercise these functions was, he said, "the Lord's reaction to the poor performance of my predecessors, who had caused the faithful to lose confidence because of their carelessness—or more precisely, their neglect of the Lord's work." On top of all that, in 2007 François Mbuyi was consecrated as deacon of the congregation. As a deacon, he is called to keep the property and funds and to keep the church records. François has an ease with statistics and reports. Without thinking or referring to documents, he can tell you that Kasekeyi CEM has "eighty-five members and a hundred-thirty children."

François Mbuyi was married to Ngalula, and together they had six children. In 2008 he married a second wife. Because of this, Pastor Tshibangu Munanga stripped him of the right to preach the word of God.

The unilateral decision took François by surprise. Although it violates a rule of the Anabaptists, François believes that having two wives cannot in any way silence a gift. However, as a child of God, he ended up submitting to the orders of the leader of the congregation, who he believes has the duty to apply the doctrine and laws of the church. But Mbuyi still is not convinced that the word of God has recorded that the Lord withdraws a gift, whatever it may be, from one who has married two or more women.

Nevertheless, he acknowledges that having the gift to teach the word of God does not mean he should be ordained either elder or pastor. In fact, François asserts that the Lord does not want him to be ordained. "If God does not want to make me pastor, I am unable to make myself pastor; and if I managed to have two wives in my life, it may be because God does not want me to serve as a pastor."

Needless to say, this incident created a stir among the faithful. François experienced other difficulties as well, related to his role as the treasurer of the congregation. He says he has been the object of slander by those who envied his position. He has been accused of diverting money from the parish or of being behind those responsible for doing so.

Despite these accusations, François remains constant in faith in God and to this day remains a member of the congregation where he served for fourteen years as congregational secretary and treasurer. "Those who know we are reliable in what we do testify to it, and are also pleased with the reports that we present," he says. "When it is said of me that I have worked well, I feel that both God and men are pleased. And it is my joy to contribute to the sustainability of the work of the Most High."

François believes that because he is in God's service, God protects him and his family and blesses his undertakings. It is thanks to God, François recognizes, that he and his household were spared after being struck by lightning. "The Lord saved me, for I was struck, my house and all my property burned, but my wife, my children, and I got out safely." François also credits the Lord for bringing him through a serious traffic accident, in which several people were killed, with only a broken arm.

He states that he has a firm faith, because "when problems arise in my ministries, I have the courage to say yes or no, when necessary, to such and such actions of men." He recognizes the hand of the Eternal in his work and plans, "protecting me against all the arrows of the devil."

Jean Félix Chimbalanga

86 ❧ Dénis Muamba's gift for sharing

Dénis Muamba Tshishimbi is director of the primary school sponsored by the Evangelical Mennonite Church (CEM) in Bufuki. Dénis is not a man of means, but he has a gift for enthusiastically sharing everything God puts into his hands.

One time, for example, he reached into his own pockets for the transportation and hosting costs of a delegation of the CEM Leadership Committee to the Bufuki congregation, when the parish failed to gather the needed resources. The instances of his generosity are legion, and all visitors to Bufuki have been the recipients of it. His pastor at Bufuki says, "Muamba Tshishimbi is a child of God who has a keen sense of sharing. All visitors to the Bufuki congregation are his personal guests. He is the man on whom the congregation and I count. He gives with a joyful heart."

Born in 1966 to Presbyterian parents in Mwene Ditu, about 130 kilometers from Mbuji Mayi, Dénis Muamba Tshishimbi confessed the faith of his parents. After primary school, he registered at the CEM's pedagogical institute and was baptized into the CEM's Bufuki congregation in Mwene Ditu. In 1994 he became director of the Bufuki Primary School, a position he holds to this day. He has also served as president of the young people and president of the laity in the Bondoyi missionary district.

Dénis has inspired others to be generous. He engaged congregation members in providing assistance to a member who lost a child,

---

photo—Dénis Muamba

as well as to Pastor Célestin Kabengela[1] following the consecutive deaths of two of his children and his grandson. As president of the laity of Bondoyi district, Dénis conducted similar actions, including a "worship walk" in which he and his administration were able to assist a struggling member in an outlying congregation.

As youth president from 1990 to 2000, Dénis Muamba mentored and supported young people as partners. He offered soap to the unemployed in order to attract them to his congregation. For those young people who became interested in the word of God, Dénis organized a campaign to promote their integration into the congregation. He established a youth choir to sing in Sunday services. Unfortunately, his leadership has not been matched since, and many of the youth have now gone elsewhere in the absence of dedicated mentoring.

The qualities of a conscientious Christian are evident in Dénis Muamba's exercise of his functions as director of the CEM Bufuki Primary School. With more than 1,500 students, it is the largest of the CEM primary schools. All is well in the management of goods and staff and in the implementation of large projects. He was responsible for the construction of the school building with six doors. He is also responsible for the clean, neat appearance of the courtyard of the Bufuki congregation where the school is located.

It is a miracle of God, he says himself, that he became director of the school. A previous director had deserted the school, leaving it leaderless and inactive for two years. Dénis cannot say exactly what prompted him to bring his fellow teachers and some students and their parents together to resume the school's activities. Today the school is stable and sustainable. Also thanks to Dénis, most of the staff are servants of God and members of the church. Quarterly evangelistic services are held at the school.

Justifying his stance of generosity, Dénis acknowledges that according to the teachings he received, the layperson is called to share what he has with others, like Jesus Christ. In sharing, he says, "I also am blessed."

One day, he recalls, he received a phone call announcing the visit of dignitaries to his school. Such visitors would have to be hosted, and this always requires money. However, Dénis had only 5,000 Congolese francs on hand, about enough to buy a single rooster. More-

1 See "Saved from suicide by a vision" (chapter 70).

over, the money had been intended for the rations of his own household, which included many children. But Dénis asked his wife to go buy a rooster for their guests, and dinner was offered to the visitors.

Two days after the visitors had eaten and returned home, Dénis received a phone call from one of his sons, whom he had not seen for many years. The son gave him the code to retrieve $100 at the bank. Dénis told his wife, Monique, "This is how God does things. The day before yesterday we spent all we had for the visitors. Now today your son sends us $100."

After retrieving the money, Dénis went home, amazed at the blessing received from God. He says, "God has rewarded me many times that way."

Jean Félix Chimbalanga

87 ⚜ Pillar of an unstable church

Monique Mutala was born into a Catholic family and married a Presbyterian, Albert Kambemba, in 1952, when she was just fourteen. Monique was only able to complete a few early years of elementary school. During her married life with Albert, she chose to become Presbyterian like her spouse. Together they had nine children, one of whom passed away.

The family eventually settled in Kabuela, where there was no Presbyterian church, so they became members of the Kasekeyi congregation of the Evangelical Mennonite Church. Albert also taught the word of God there, having been ordained pastor in the place from which he came. Albert died in 1992.

It was in 1998 that Monique Mutala became fully active in this congregation where she had become involved bit by bit. She became president of the women of the congregation. As a leader, Monique was characterized by zeal and enthusiasm. She herself declares the joy she experienced when everyone worked together in harmony to help the needy both in the congregation and in the local community. Monique was a great mobilizer. For example, she led the women in planting a manioc field measuring fifty square meters, from which nearly half the produce was sold and its income presented to the congregation to help purchase a sound system. She also brought a number of women to Christ during her eleven years as president of the women.

---

photo—Monique Mutala

Mama Monique demonstrated exceptional bravery and courage. Others didn't always listen to her or agree with her. Some accused her of being a dictator. She was often the object of gossip. In spite of all that, she remained connected to God, whose servant she is, and never dared give up her duties that the congregation entrusted to her. After she left the presidency of the group, she became its treasurer. In the face of the diminishing offerings and the falling away of the mothers in their service for God with their goods, Monique took it on herself to exhort them to participate in the work of the Lord with all that they received from their labors.

Monique is one of the rare mothers whose children all worship with her in her own church, where they all have responsibilities as influential members and servants of God. Mama Mutala recognizes unequivocally that it is the Lord who called her children to his service: "I was not capable of converting my children to God and making them his servants." She recognizes, however, that as a mother, each time she herself went to church, she always took care to bring them along. Monique reminds others repeatedly and with conviction of the Baluba proverb that says a child can never ignore who his parents are, because at their death this identity will be left to the child.

Trusting firmly in God, Mama Monique attests that the stability that she and her children experience, despite her widowhood, is the work of the Eternal himself, who has blessed her and her children in their studies, with stable marriages, and with children. Monique Mutala believes she has contributed to the growth of the Kasekeyi congregation not only by evangelizing women but also by adding her own children, their spouses, and her grandchildren. Monique expresses great joy in having served her God, and she believes the blessings that accompany her in her life are a reward from God for having served him in these ways.

But she is concerned about the well-being of her congregation. She deplores its poor management by a succession of pastors, who she says are not disposed to facilitate its growth. Monique observes with regret that these individuals are driving away the faithful rather than gathering them in, and she notes that most of those who leave are the women. Nevertheless, she continues to multiply her exhortations to them with the goal of renewing the unity and fellowship of the community.

She hopes that church authorities might send her congregation responsible leaders who will be concerned about its longevity and its development. "My fondest wish for CEM Kasekeyi is that, even though it is very unstable and always faced with problems of the sort that work against its progress—it has otherwise been very remarkable for a very long time—the high hierarchy of the CEM would think of sending a good pastor for its rehabilitation."

Jean Félix Chimbalanga

88 ❧ Athanase Musende's last pastoral visit

Pastor Athanase Musende's voice on the other end of the call early in Easter week 2012 was quiet, yet urgent. "I can't walk!" Helpless in the face of his troubling medical condition and the distance separating us, I could only appeal to the Great Physician.

"We'll pray for you," I offered, overwhelmed with the significance of the fact that he had called me. Two years of trying to get help for him had not yielded the results we had hoped for. He was suffering from severe heart disease.

"Thank you!" he said simply, and then the call was dropped. I tried again and again to call back but couldn't make the connection between Kinshasa, where I was, and Pastor Musende in Kamayala, where I had known him since my childhood as the daughter of missionaries Ben and Helen Eidse.

Later I was on the phone with Wenyi Nzey', an elder of the congregation, and I asked about Pastor Musende. Could he walk?

"He's still walking, but with difficulty," said Wenyi.

However, a few days later, at 12:30 on Holy Saturday morning, April 7, Pastor Musende died in his footsteps, so to speak. He had given the Easter week seminars every day at the Kamayala church, expounding the death and resurrection of Christ, comparing it with the human experience of death. "You have to endure suffering in

photo—Athanase Musende (first adult on left), with friends Dénis Kamanda, Mavula Kutaha, and Jacques Kamanda order to experience resurrection," he said, and cited the account of Joseph and his brothers.

"He spoke with special insight, as if from personal experience," said Wenyi Nzey'. "He interspersed the teaching with songs filled with pathos. We were astounded and moved to tears."

Wenyi reported that after the Kamalaya Good Friday service, Pastor Musende had borrowed his motorbike to visit a village four kilometers away, administered baptism and communion, and then returned home. "During the week he told me once that he couldn't sleep at night and wondered if he would live until morning," Wenyi told me. "We realize now that God extended his life through this week so he could impart this teaching." The news of his death shook the region and the Mennonite Church of Congo (CMCo) community. Pastor Musende was in his late fifties.

Justin Mbuyuyu, son of a pastor who had worked with my father, was the new pastor of that village. The baptismal candidates were the first fruits of his ministry. Justin spoke passionately of his vision for growth in the village and church. "I know I have resisted becoming a pastor my whole life," he told me. "I never wanted to be poor like my parents were. But I know now that this is my calling. I am ready to follow Christ, no matter what the sacrifice." Pastor Musende's last sacrificial act, his taking each painful step in order to administer baptism in Justin's congregation, will have an enduring result.

Pastor Musende was a repository of history, Chokwe culture, and language. A nephew of pastor Emmanuel Wayindama,[1] he knew all the original pastors, their gifts, and works. He was an expert in Anabaptist theology, a skilled peacemaker. He was a calm man of few words and a ready smile. Whenever he did speak, it was with wisdom and insight. He served Kamayala and Kahemba districts as a Bible institute professor, a high school teacher, and a key pastor and spiritual leader. He did not seek high position or power and had turned down the nomination as head of the district. A singer with a beautiful voice, he was the one who knew all the songs in the Chokwe hymn book.

In spite of his heavy teaching and preaching load, Pastor Musende farmed and worked hard in his dry-season market gardens.

---

1 See "A small man of giant wisdom" (chapter 24), and "That's all you can do to me" (chapter 26).

He provided for his wife and extended family. He was a loving husband, father, friend, and mentor, a victorious and dedicated Christian.

"One thing in particular stands out about him," said Wenyi. "He never despaired, even in these last years of suffering."

In his death as in his life, Pastor Musende Uthu Naweji Athanase demonstrated the transcendent power of the resurrection. As we stood on the threshold of heaven on Easter weekend, we relinquished our brother to the One who gives and who takes away. We persevered to say, "I know that my Redeemer lives!"

Charity Eidse Schellenberg

⁂ Acknowledgments

I'm grateful to God for these stories, which demonstrate how the Spirit has touched many Congolese lives over the past century, leading to strong Mennonite communities. God's forgiving and empowering grace shines through in a variety of ways in these glimpses of individuals, who through faith in Jesus have made a strong impact in the life of the church. To God be the glory!

Thanks to my wife, Lynda. Your constant encouragement and belief in the value of this work have made a huge difference.

This project would have remained a great idea and no more, but for the many persons in both Congo and North America who gave time, skills, energy, ideas, and funds to help make it happen. Thanks for sharing your gifts out of your passion, your love for the church, and your generosity.

AIMM's ambassador emeritus, the ninety-years-young Dr. James Bertsche, with the faithful support of his wife, Jenny, has provided major impetus for accomplishing this project all the way along. The idea itself emerged from conversation with Jim. He organized and led most of the fundraising for the project, employing his contacts, setting up meetings, and making presentations over an eighteen-month period. His prodigious memory and storytelling skill contributed to a number of stories included in this collection. Jim served twenty-five years as a missionary in Congo and twelve years as administrator of AIMM. He wrote the history of the mission, *CIM/AIMM: A Story of Vision, Commitment, and Grace.* His personal knowledge and experience of the history of Congo Inland Mission/Africa Inter-Mennonite Mission and the Congo churches that emerged from its work became an important touchstone during the editing process both in Congo and North America. Jim, thank you. What an immense privilege it's been to work with you.

Thanks to Mennonite Church of Congo President Rev. Dr. Adolphe Komuesa Kalunga and Evangelical Mennonite Church of Congo President Rev. Benjamin Mubenga Wa Kabanga. Your enthusiasm, support, management ideas, and knowledge of your communities have all been keys to the success of this undertaking.

Congolese researchers Jackson Mwatha Beleji, Robert Sakayimbo Chibulenu, Jean Félix Chimbalanga Wa Mpoyi, Gregoire Moele Djenke Kaumba, Jean Bosco Musakai, Salomon Luku Sa Muya, and Dominique Yona dedicated months of their time and energy to travel widely, visiting many congregations in order to record oral interviews with church members concerning their own or others' lives and ministries. More than 500 local-language interviews have been recorded and preserved. You gathered the foundational information that the writers drew on to write this book. Thanks for your work.

Historian Dr. Fohle Lygunda led the research team in a several-day orientation, sharing essential guidelines on conducting oral interviews and working with the team to identify individuals for whom information needed to be gathered. Thanks, Dr. Fohle.

Congolese writers led by Vincent Mulebo Ndandula, along with Jean Félix Chimbalanga Wa Mpoyi and Jackson Mwatha Beleji, combined their multiple language capabilities with French language literary skill, historical and spiritual insight, and passion for the subject at hand, in order to produce most of these "picture-stories." Thank you for sharing your gifts through these stories. Thanks to Charity Eidse Schellenberg for your beautiful story on Pastor Musende.

Thanks to Nancy Myers, truly a gift of God, who offered her Congo experience, French language capability, and considerable editorial skills on a completely volunteer basis for this volume, at exactly the right time. In addition to editing all the English and already translated stories, she combined skills in translation and editing in order to produce many of the finished stories. She also took charge of the structure of the book, laying out the stories' order, and getting it done on time. Nancy, we could not have achieved this without you.

The translation team did a fine job of rendering French stories into English, often on a volunteer basis. Thanks so much for your contributions to this project. Principal translators were Sylvia Shirk and Sharon Hewitt, accompanied by Nancy Frey and Dr. Jeremy Rich.

Thanks to Dr. James Krabill of Mennonite Mission Network for your encouragement for this project and your willingness to help connect it to Institute of Mennonite Studies.

Thanks to Institute of Mennonite Studies at Anabaptist Mennonite Biblical Seminary for accepting this book for publication. Thanks particularly to Barbara Nelson Gingerich, whose encouragement, knowledge of book publishing, contacts, and organizing skills have helped to keep us on track and to make large tasks doable. Thanks to James Nelson Gingerich for his gift of formatting.

Dr. Jan Bender Shetler, professor of African history at Goshen College, has extensive experience with the oral interview process in Africa and shared practical advice that made a positive difference in the quality of this book. Dr. Jon Bonk of the Overseas Ministries Study Centre, besides encouraging this project, connected me with Dr. Fohle, who in turn provided high quality training for the research team. Dr. John Roth of Goshen College's Institute for the Study of Global Anabaptism offered constant encouragement for sharing these stories. Thanks to all of you.

Thanks to my work colleagues—AIMM office manager Lola Gingerich, Steve Wiebe-Johnson of Mennonite Mission Network, and Hippolyto Tshimanga of Mennonite Church Canada. Your work and support for this project have been significant.

Rod Hollinger-Janzen
AIMM Executive Coordinator

ॐ Appendix

Terms, history, and background

Mission names

The Congo Inland Mission (CIM) was founded by two small Mennonite groups in central Illinois in 1912. Over time, missionary candidates applied from other areas, and the supporting base of CIM broadened. By the 1950s and 1960s the CIM board included representatives from six different North American Mennonite conferences.

In 1972, following the conclusion of a fusion of mission and church in the Congo, the CIM board opted to change the name to Africa Inter-Mennonite Mission (AIMM).

AIMM area geography

The Illinois-sized area for which the CIM accepted evangelizing responsibility in 1912 is located in south-central Congo. In the north it skirts rain forests; in the south it recedes into rolling savannah and touches the Angolan border. Three major rivers cross this area from south to north—the Kasai River in the east, the Kwilu River in the west, and the Loange River, which makes its way through the central Mennonite area. All three rivers eventually converge in the Congo River. The volume of water the Congo River discharges into the Atlantic is second only to that of the Amazon of South America.

The languages of Congo

As there are hundreds of ethnic groups within the borders of the Congo (equal in size to the United States east of the Mississippi), so are there hundreds of dialects. Over time, four major tribal languages have come to dominate the linguistic landscape: Swahili in eastern Congo; Tshiluba in Congo's heartland; Kikongo in the western part of the country; and Lingala, the language of the tribe from which President Mobutu came in northwestern Congo, which became the language of the military. Tshiluba became the language used by CIM/AIMM missionaries along the Kasai River. Otherwise missionaries sought to learn and use the language of the people among whom they lived and served.

Urban centers of the Congo

As far as the work of CIM/AIMM was concerned, four urban centers were important: Kinshasa, the capital (called Leopoldville by the Belgians), followed by Kikwit to the west, Kananga (Luluabourg to the Belgians) to the east, and Tshikapa centrally located to the mission area. Mbuji Mayi, the capital of then–South Kasai, was the center for the refugee church that emerged after independence (see the section on Mennonite church names below).

Belgian administrative structures

The Belgians divided the entire country into a handful of large provinces over which there were Belgian "governors." Each province was then divided into "territories," over which there were Belgian "administrators." Then came "sectors," over which African chiefs were chosen and appointed by Belgians to preside according to their local village customs. A number of stories in this book deal with Mennonite Christians who were appointed to such roles after political independence.

Eight CIM/AIMM mission posts

1912 Ndjoko Punda (Charlesville) among the Lulua, Baluba, and Bakuba people

1913 Kalamba among the Lulua people (relocated eight miles to the west to Mutena in 1964)

1921 Nyanga among the eastern Pende

1923 Mukedi among the western Pende

1950 Banga among the Lele and Wongo

1950 Kalonda overlooking the Tshikapa government/commercial center among the Chokwe, Pende, Lulua, and Baluba

1953 Kamayala (acquired from the Unevangelized Tribes Missions (UTM)) among the Chokwe and Lunda

1954 Kandala (acquired from an independent Canadian Baptist couple, Percival and Rosalind Near) among the southern Pende and Sonde

CIM/AIMM schools

Helping Africans across the threshold of literacy so they could enroll in a variety of educational programs was an early and enduring goal of the mission. Across time, educational opportunities the mission offered took many forms.

- primary schools, grades 1–6, followed by several options:
- two-year teacher training programs for lower primary levels
- two-year preparatory study for secondary schools
- four-year teacher training programs for teaching and supervisory roles
- four-year high school leading to university level study
- training for pastors and leaders
- two-year post-primary Bible study for village evangelists
- a four-year Bible Institute established at Kalonda in 1953
- a joint three-year pastoral training program established with the Mennonite Brethren Mission in 1963 at their mission post Kajiji on the Angolan border
- a merger of the above program with a similar American Baptist school in 1968 eventually located in Kinshasa
- vocational training
- two-year vocational training programs in woodworking and masonry
- a four-year training program for girls in design and sewing
- on-the-job training of nurses, midwives, and surgical assistants

Mennonite church names

In this book we refer to two main churches, the Mennonite Church of Congo (CMCo) and the Evangelical Mennonite Church of Congo (CEM). But the history of these names and the churches themselves is complicated.

Initially there was a single Mennonite church known as the Evangelical Mennonite Church of the Congo. With the advent of General Mobutu, this church was known as Communauté Mennonite du Zaïre (CMZa). With his overthrow in 1997 the name reverted to Communauté Mennonite du Congo (CMCo). The term *communauté* (community) is used to signify that the Mennonites, like all other Congo Protestant denominations, are members of a single overarching Church of Christ of Congo. In this book we call the CMCo the Mennonite Church of Congo. We use the French acronym CMCo because it is commonly used in Congo (pronounced "sem-co").

When Congo acquired its political independence in June of 1960, a long-simmering animosity between the Lulua and Baluba people along the Kasai River erupted into violence which triggered a migration of the Baluba to their ancestral homeland in the South Kasai. This migration, described in a number of stories in Part III, took a large group of Mennonite leaders and members with it. Cut off from the mother church by distance and political cleavage, these refugees eventually established a second Mennonite church, which was eventually named the Communauté Evangélique Mennonite or CEM ("sem")—called in this book the Evangelical Mennonite Church.

A third Mennonite Church exists in Congo today, which stems indirectly from the work of CIM/AIMM. Aaron and Ernestina Janzen were early pioneers who served with Congo Inland Mission. After several terms they became aware of a large area to the west of CIM territory where there was no evangelical witness. Of Mennonite Brethren background, they generated some support at home and returned to pioneer a new work in the Kikwit area. Following World War II the Mennonite Brethren Conference assumed support for this work. The church born of this witness and ministry is today known as the Communauté des Eglises de Frères Mennonites du Congo (CEFMC; Mennonite Brethren Churches of Congo).

Today the CMCo and the CEFMC number about 100,000 members each, while the CEM numbers about 23,000.[1]

---

1 For a brief history of each of these groups, see these articles: James E. Bertsche, "Communauté Mennonite au Congo," *Global Anabaptist Mennonite Encyclopedia Online*; http://www.gameo.org/encyclopedia/contents/C654035.html; James E. Bertsche, "Communauté Evangélique Mennonite (Democratic Republic of Congo)," *Global Anabaptist Mennonite Encyclopedia Online*; http://www.gameo.org/encyclopedia/contents/C654033.html; A. E. Janzen and Peter M. Hamm, "Communauté des Eglises de Frères Mennonites au Congo," *Global Anabaptist Mennonite Encyclopedia Online*; http://www.gameo.org/encyclopedia/contents/C65403.html.

Congo church structures and terminology

Originally eight large church districts were named for the mission posts around which they had developed. As the church grew and as Africans took over self-governance, these districts were broken down into numerous smaller subdistricts. It is the intent that they all be supervised and led by an ordained pastor, although shortage of personnel does not always make this possible.

Annual assemblies bring together representatives from across these districts for discussion, planning, devotional studies, and decision making.

Each congregation, district, and denomination has an elected president/legal representative, a vice-president/legal representative, a treasurer, and a recording secretary, plus a variety of other positions as the church may decide. The term *legal representative* refers to the person who conducts any and all business with the government on behalf of the church—for instance, regarding land, schools, and hospitals. This position is required by the Congolese government, as it was by the colonial government.

Titles used in Congo churches frequently include pastor in chief (lead pastor), elder, deacon, evangelist, intercessor (prayer coordinator), youth animator, and choir director. As is clear from many of these stories, women have their own congregational, district, and national organizations and positions.

Some of the stories of this book reflect rivalries and frictions. Yet mature leaders have brought about reconciliation, often at the price of yielding authority to which they were entitled.

Names and traditions

Baptism among Congolese Mennonites is by immersion, and it follows a period of biblical orientation, declaration of faith, and observation of daily life. The one being baptized usually wears new clothing, and traditionally he or she adopted a new name to add to their village name. Frequently these names are of biblical origin. Thus Falanga becomes Falanga Elie, and Gavunji becomes Gavunji Rebecca. Now Christian names are often given at birth.

We have simplified the names in this book and arranged them in the usual English order. Congolese usually put the Christian name last, following an African given name and family name: Kabasela Mbaya André. The African given name (Kabasela) is treated as a person's principal name in most situations and is often conferred according to an elaborate system of succession and relationship. The family name (Mbaya) is less significant than it is in Western societies. In this book we have eliminated most family names and put the Christian name first (André Kabasela). Women usually keep their own names after marriage.

Evangelism continues to be a strong theme among the Congo Mennonites. Where the church is growing, messages are direct and uncompromising: "Apart from the saving grace of Jesus, we are all lost sinners. But we have good news! You need no longer live in daily fear of the threatening world of dangerous spirits of our forefathers. Jesus changed all of that when he died on a cross and walked out of his tomb three days later!"

As these stories reveal, Mennonite Christians in Congo are subject to foibles, failures, and sins, as are the North American sons and daughters of Menno. But their stories are a reminder that God has a way of honoring simple prayers of penitence and a faithful witness to his name.

—The Editors